Song

Apply Proven Methods, Ideas and Exercises to Kickstart or Upgrade Your Songwriting

Table of Contents

Introduction	6
Chapter 1: Understanding the Basics	8
Chapter 2: Don't Wait For Inspiration	12
Chapter 3: What is your topic and genre?	17
Chapter 4: Working with Collaborators	31
Chapter 5: Use the Five Senses	37
Chapter 6: Starting With a Melody	45
Chapter 7: Chords, Keys, and Progressions	70
The Note	70
The Chord	71
Chord Progressions	72
Playing With Chord Progressions	73
CHAPTER 8: DEALING WITH INSPIRATION	77
Capturing Inspiration	77
Encouraging Inspiration	80
CHAPTER 9: SINGING WITH SYLLABLES, A WAY TO FIND YOUR RHYTHM	82
CHAPTER 10: ADD SOME BACKGROUND VOICES	87
CHAPTER 11: ADD SOME MOVEMENTS TO THE PROCESS	91
CHAPTER 12: AVOID THE TURN-OFFS	94
CHAPTER 13: IT'S A NUMBERS GAME	99
CHAPTER 14: DO I NEED A PUBLISHER?	105
CHAPTER 15: FIND THE THEME TO YOUR SONG	112

CHAPTER 16: ADJUST THE WORDING TO THE RHYTHM 121

CHAPTER 17: CREATIVITY 125

Creativity With Form 125

Creativity With Lyrics 128

Creativity With Music 131

CHAPTER 18: BECOME A PROFESSIONAL SONGWRITER 136

What Does It Take? 136

Rights, Royalties, And Piracy 138

Professional Songwriter Habits 145

You Should Write Every Single Day 145

Pro Songwriters Know Their Strengths 147

CHAPTER 19: DO I NEED TO COPYRIGHT MY SONGS? 150

CHAPTER 20: SONG OUTLETS – GET OUT OF THE BOX! 175

CHAPTER 21: BUILD YOUR ONLINE PRESENCE 187

CHAPTER 22: THE LITTLE THINGS 192

CHAPTER 23: MORE TIPS 196

Types of Songs 196

Do You Write the Lyrics Before or After the Music? 199

Turn Your Title Into Lyrics 203

Use Your Motivation To Bring Your Song To Life 206

Find a Structure For Your Song 209

Find The Melody in Your Lyrics	211
How to Improve Your Songwriting Skills	212
CHAPTER 24: FITTING IT IN AN HOUR	214
CHAPTER 25: POLISHING	222
Conclusion	225

Discover "How to Find Your Sound"

HTTP://MUSICPROD.ONTRAPAGES.COM/

SWINDALI MUSIC COACHING/SKYPE LESSONS.

Email djswindali@gmail.com for info and pricing

INTRODUCTION

Writing songs has sometimes been known for being hard and very complicated to do. Some people get very frustrated and don't have a single clue of what to do after they try to write a song or just a single verse. This happens to a lot of people, because in a way, songwriting is a talent. But the good news is that we all have the talent; the difference is that a few works to develop and improve it, and others do not. So, all you have to do is improve your skills.

Obviously, no one is born with the talent at its best. All famous songwriters have become recognized, because little by little, they have improved their songwriting skills. How? By practicing and experimenting until they get what they want. And everyone can do it as well. You only need some advice and a little help, and you will see that songwriting has suddenly become a whole lot easier for you.

The most important aspect of songwriting is learning to be patient. Don't get frustrated and quit too early, because nobody has ever gotten anywhere quitting when things get a little complicated. Stay focused and be persistent if you can't write an entire song in just one sitting or, at least, not a great one. You can only get better with time.

"Every child is an artist, with imagination and the artistic instinct. Life stamps these out..." -- Percy Mack

It is important to use your strengths instead of torturing yourself with things you are not good at doing. Songwriting should be fun!

Chapter 1: Understanding the Basics

While anyone can write song lyrics, this process tends to flow much more smoothly if you have a basic idea of how most songs are structured. Your song can include all or none of the suggestions outlined below, there are no wrong answers.

- *Introduction*: The opening section of a song can sometimes be significantly different from the rest in terms of style, tone or rhythm. Many songs do not have an introduction, consider it only if you feel your song needs one.
- *Verse:* The majority of your lyrics will be split into verses which tend to each be roughly twice the length of the chorus. While the words change from verse to verse, their patterns and themes should be the same. If every song is a story, the verse is the part of the story that pushes the action forward.
- *Chorus:* This is the part of your song that will repeat, generally once or twice either verbatim or with minor changes. Many musicians put their most memorable lyrics, referred to as the hook, in the chorus. Think of the chorus as the overall theme or message that your song is trying to portray.
- *Bridge:* This is another element that is present in some songs but not in others. It is typically quite short, and placed after the chorus has repeated at least once and will often be followed by a change in key. Story wise, it is an opportunity to look at things from another perspective.

Common song structure

When it comes to structuring your song, the most commonly used structures are referred to as forms and written as ABC. In this case "A" is used to represent a verse, "B" is used to represent a chorus and "C" represents the bridge.

AABA form: The most common song structure sees two verses, followed by a chorus and then a final verse. Written as AABA, this was the primary song form of choice prior to 1960. In this case the A's are verses while the B's represents the bridge of the song. An extended version of this form is what is known as AABABA and includes a second bridge and an additional verse which can also be another complete verse or part of a verse

Another common trope of this form is to repeat the name of the song in each verse in roughly the same place. Use the bridge to give the song some contrast by possibly switching the focus of the song briefly or otherwise bridging the previous verses with the final one. The last verse can be the same as the first verse in this song form. While it has decreased in popularity in the past few decades, AABA is still used regularly in the theatre as well as in jazz, pop, Christian, gospel and country songs.

AAAA form: If you have a poem you are looking to put to music, then this is the form for you. Each time the musical melody repeats, the words change. This form often features refrains at the end of each verse that tends to repeat the same line each time, and often contain the title as well. This is one of the oldest types of songs and it originated in medieval Europe. This is the easiest type of song to write if you are looking to tell a story.

AB form: If you are looking to write a song that alternates between verses and chorus, then look no further. This is the main form used by songwriters since the 1960s. While other forms place the majority of their focus on the verses, in AB form that emphasis is reversed. Rather, the chorus is emphasized while also containing the core message of the song and frequently its title. In these scenarios, the verse functions to provide the buildup required to make the chorus stand out even more.

AB songs typically have around three verses and the same number of chorus breaks. It is important to try and tell a story with your verses that thematically connects to the chorus. Likewise, keep your verses short and sweet and focus on getting back to the chorus. A bridge can be added on to the AB form to create the ABC form that includes a bridge that leads into the second chorus. A version that goes ABABB, and ends with a double chorus are also popular.

Consider adding a bridge if you are looking to make your song longer, add in story points that don't fit in the verse format or if you feel your song is too repetitive and need something to break up the monotony.

Chapter 2: Don't Wait For Inspiration

Struggle through it until inspiration hits

Inspiration is an important element to songwriting. You'll have good days, when you'll get a verse and maybe the chorus done, and then there are other days, when you are stuck on that one phrase that just isn't right. Don't worry; it happens to us all. Just sit down and keep working on it. You never know when something will click, and you'll take off with a great guitar riff or lyrical verse that is exactly the way you wanted it.

Writers of all kinds have days, when they just want to throw in the towel, but the difference between them and the ones who make it is they keep trying, even when they hate what they're doing that day.

Inspiration tends to disappear just as quickly as it came. It is, therefore, important to take a moment when it comes along and create a melodic theme, idea, or phrase, or at least the song title. And what happens when the inspiration has gone? There are 2 options:

1) You put aside your theme or part of a song somewhere on a shelf, record and wait for next time when inspiration comes to continue. In this case, you're as dependent on the inspiration as on a capricious woman.

2) You keep working until the main lines of the song are finished, and you just have to make technical things to

make everything complete. In this case, you will continue to work, regardless of inspiration, and it can come again and serve you, instead of you serving it. Thanks to your habit or character, the cranky woman is tamed and increasingly visits you. Therefore, inspiration is a good thing, but character - even better.

Inspiration picks you up, but habit or character keeps you up there.

And so, it is important to establish the habit - not to depend on inspiration:

1) To be ready, when inspiration strikes you, to record your ideas on your iPhone or any other device,

2) To complete the unfinished musical ideas at least along general lines, and even though this song is nothing special, it forms your character or habit to complete unfinished works, and you will be less dependent on inspiration.

You can't get your second wind when you are standing. You can get it when you are moving.

So, waiting for inspiration is not good; instead, you should focus on making songwriting a habit you pursue daily. 15 minutes of daily writing will offer you inspiration and great lyrics, so focus on doing such a thing.

How a Song Comes into Being

Your initial idea, which you have played and recorded, will need to inspire you to proceed further in developing what may be a few seconds into a full song. A good song will bring in the listener, because it tells a story and conveys strong emotions. The listener will feel compelled to hear the song, because it relates to them on a basic level.

A good storyteller can convey the emotions and story of the song in such a manner that the listener may visualize what they hear. A good song takes you on a journey. This is why it is so important to get down your first ideas and develop them.

What are popular musicians using as inspiration?

A good story would be Eric Clapton's. He wrote "Layla" when a friend shared with him a Persian story, named The Story of Layla and Majnun, about unrequited love. It was something Eric related to, considering his unrequited love was George Harrison's wife.

On the other hand, Michael Jackson wrote "Billy Jean" as he was driving. He was so focused on writing down his ideas that the car lit on fire. People that passed near him on the road let him know about the issue.

Think about the songs you like and the ones that make it big in the charts. If you notice, many songs that stick tell a story or invoke a strong emotion. Where do you think great songwriters get their inspiration? Here are the top three sources of inspiration for songwriting:

1. Romantic Relationships

Taylor Swift is one of those artists known to have hits that pertain to her past relationships. Experiences in romantic relationships often provide enough substance to generate hits like Justin Timberlake's "Cry Me a River", Kelly Clarkson's "Stronger", and Usher's "Confessions." Sometimes, artists and songwriters can even narrate an entire relationship story (including elation over love, angst, anger, and bitterness over breakups) in several hits in one album. Remember Maroon 5's songs about Jane?

2. Going Through Difficult Times

What is the common factor between Beyoncé's "Heartbeat", Ben Folds Five's "Brick", and Ed Sheeran's "Small Bump"? They all talk about going through losing an unborn child. Coldplay's "Fix You" is supposedly dedicated to Gwyneth Paltrow, who was going through the loss of her dad, and Blake Shelton's "Over You" is about the passing of his brother in a car accident.

3. Memories

Many recording artists talk about their memories of childhood and growing up. The element of nostalgia makes for a great inspiration, and many fans are interested in knowing the past of artists and relate to them. One artist, who has written hits about his growing up experiences, includes Eminem with "Cleaning Out My Closet."

Great songwriters know how to take inspiration from almost anything they see and feel. The closer a song is to their hearts, the greater chances of it being relatable and hitting the charts.

CHAPTER 3: WHAT IS YOUR TOPIC AND GENRE?

There are strategies which you can implement to be a prolific songwriter. You do not need to be overwhelmed as you venture deeper into the field of songwriting.

If you are someone who has no music knowledge, do not be alarmed. It is not a requisite to be a great songwriter. If you have knowledge about music, then you can use what you know to help you write your song.

From time to time, your creativity may come to a halt. Everyone suffers from writer's block at some stage. Therefore, do not panic. Feed your mind and do something to distract you, rather than gazing at the wall for many hours every day.

Inspiration comes when you least expect it. If you feel like doing house chores do so. Exercise. Enjoy nature. When you feel more relaxed and calm, continue with your task. Approach songwriting systematically.

Focus on what you wish to hear rather than trying to express yourself in such a way that it needs a literature professor to decipher the song's meaning. In other words, write with your listeners in mind. You only have a few minutes to captivate your listeners' attention so ensure that the words are understood. Of course, your listeners may ascribe different meanings to your song. However, it is better to have a song that is cherished by music lovers for various reasons than have a song that is disregarded because there is no connection with your listeners at all.

Remember, the purpose of any good song is to connect with individual listeners and the way to go about doing that is by creating something that impacts them emotionally when they hear it. As such, when it comes to generating ideas for songs, it can be helpful to know what types of emotions you want to express, but only if you use that knowledge as a starting point for creating lyrics instead of the impetus for them. Once you know what you want to say, the best way to ensure that you are really connecting with people is to take the feelings behind those words and then think about what you might hear that would connect to those emotions for you.

At first, writing from a listener's perspective might be difficult, but with practice you will find that it comes easier and easier, this is what is known as writing with a listener's ear. Eventually, you can tweak your lyrics but have your listeners in mind. Your major focus shouldn't be on winning national or international awards either. When you start to focus on extraneous matters, it's like trying to jump over an obstacle without first gathering momentum.

Everything is a process. To get outside, you first have to open your door. You do not snap your fingers and like magic, you are outside. Though writing can take you into the fantasy realm, always be mindful that in reality you will have to dedicate the time and work. It won't all come together in an instant. Take everything in stride. Before you can win awards, you first have to write a compelling and fabulous song.

Topics

Let us examine a few topics which you can write about.

Moving Characters

Many hit songs focus on unforgettable characters. Is there someone who captures your attention? What about the person captivates you? What about someone's character can motivate you to write? What is your character's heartfelt desire? What conflict is your character trying to resolve or overcome?

Think of your high school crush or anyone who you secretly admire. If you had to express to a friend why that person makes your heart palpitate, what would you say?

Be free with your imagination. Make the words come more excitingly alive. What about the people in your neighborhood? Do you have a muttering Matt, a sassy Sally, or a scoundrel André in your area? What makes these people so different from the others? Though you may not be aware of their personal details, if you have to craft a story what would you convey? Was sassy Sally once a shy girl? What is Matt always muttering about? Is he always discriminated for a flaw or does he mutter to distract himself from the scary thoughts in his head? Is André really a scoundrel or is that a tough persona and he is really a nice guy? Be more imaginative and creative with your topics.

The people you love

If you could express to someone why you love him or her without saying "I love you," what would you say? Imagine that in every tender moment those three words vanish from your vocabulary and you need other words to express how you feel. How would you convey your feelings?

If it is a romantic relationship, did you always love the person? If not, what caused you to change your mind? Did you have the wrong perception of the person or did the person undergo a transformation?

Your personal life

If you are reading this book, it means that you have a unique way of communicating. I'm also sure that there are situations in your current life or that happened before, that caused your friends and family to view you differently. Reflect for a moment. What stories have you shared at gatherings that either left your friends in shock or break out with peals of laughter? Those stories may not only be good for social gatherings but I'm sure you can pen some lyrics based on your ordeal.

Fantasies

If you could do anything that defies logic, human intellect, and the laws of nature what would it be?

Common Themes

Write about the emotions that we all go through: betrayal, falling in love, heartbreak, losing someone, anger, or depression. If you are not necessarily enduring any of these emotions, think about the people who have endured them and write about it

Sing the Blues

Rather than just feeling or singing the blues, write about it. Channel your creativity when you feel under the weather and sad.

Tragedy

You can write about a traumatic topic. What would you say to someone who is trying to manage his or her life after enduring adversities?

Infidelity

Infidelity comes with many emotions not just by the aggrieved party but also the one who is sneaking around. The guilt of what is done, the secrets and pretending, all take a toll. You can explore infidelity from different angles.

Nostalgic for the past

Everyone wishes he or she could return to something in his or her past. If you had to return to your past, what would be your motivating factor to take that journey?

Apologizing

When we are angry and hasty with our words, after we are calmer, we wish we could take them back. Since we cannot take them back, only the right apology and a forgiving heart can redeem us. Many people wish to express the right words but don't know how. Pen the lyrics to a song so that when people are clueless about what to say to the person they have offended, they can sing the song instead or play your song.

Look at what is trending in the media

You can also obtain ideas about what is trending in the media. Are there sporting events taking place? Is there chaos or more order after an election? Is there an economic crisis? Has a hurricane hit a country? Did a famous couple split? Did a celebrity die?

Keep your ears attuned

Sometimes a phrase someone says may induce a creative spark. Therefore, keep your ears attentive for unusual expressions and quotes. Ensure that you obtain permission when it is needed.

Feminine themes

There is the angelic demure female personality you can write about or the feisty woman who can do anything a man can do and even better. You can also write empowerment themes. For example, look at the lyrics of the song "I Will Survive."

Locale

What is distinct about the area where you reside or the town or country? What notable landmarks are there? Consider the song "Girl from Ipanema."

Ask questions and give answers

You can also ask questions and give listeners the answers.

Holidays and Seasons

Despite all the Christmas hits, there is always room for one more song. You can also focus on other holidays and the seasons.

Now that you have these ideas, make a note of the topics that inspire you. Also, brainstorm for other topics that you wish to explore.

Genre

There are various types of songs. Some songs can be classified in more than one genre. These are the more important ones but note that the list is not exhaustive.

Classical

Classical songs are those where traditional music is a key component. Artists such as Wolfgang Amadeus Mozart composed classical songs.

Pop

Pop songs have a cheerful rhythm with contemporary words.

Rock 'n' Roll

Rock 'n' Roll commonly referred to as Rock developed with the arrival of the electric guitar. Distinct in the songs are the bass guitar, drums, keyboards and of course the lead guitar. The Rolling Stones and The Beatles are two prominent bands that played this type of music.

Metal

Metal songs are harsher than rock. The songs incorporate elevated pitches and high-pitched vocals.

Country

Country music can be traced back to folk music. In the 18th and 19 centuries, settlers from England, Ireland and Scotland settled in the southern parts of the USA. The folk songs are the foundation for country songs.

The songs usually have a slow tempo. Many popular country songs focus on love and heartache. Instruments used mainly consist of the harmonica, banjo, acoustic and steel guitar.

In the 1940s, many record labels were formed in Nashville Tennessee and from thereon Nashville has been the base for country music. If this is the type of music you wish to focus on, you should know the popular country and western songs and examine the lyrics.

Rap or Hip-Hop

Lyrics are usually recited over a rhythm. You should have a flair for penning the various types of rhymes.

Ballads

These are songs with narration of a story being executed musically. It is a love song with a slow or moderate tempo.

Dance

These songs are fast and have an infectious rhythm structure. They are played at parties and clubs. One example is Kylie Minogue's song "Can't Get You Out of My Head."

Love songs

These songs focus on love and the interworking of relationships.

Gospel songs

The lyrics are biblically based and adhere to the Christian tradition. They are based on experiences one has with God, trials and how to overcome them.

Rhythm and Blues

Rhythm and Blues is also referred to as R & B or R 'n' B. African American artists first performed this genre but now it is popularized around the world. There are elements of pop, funk music and soul music. Hip and hop is now added and when this occurs it is referred to as contemporary R & B.

Listen to classic songs such as "The Great Pretenders" and "Only You" by The Platters. Know the pioneers of this form of music such as Chuck Berry and Muddy Waters. Do not limit what you listen to, only to your contemporaries.

There are various hybrids and variations but these are the main types of songs. You need to decide what type of song you are going to write and know what theme you have in mind.

Writing for commercials

Another factor which you can take into consideration is writing for commercials. When doing so, there are certain matters which you must take into consideration. These are what must be analyzed:

- Who is your targeted group? Are you catering to children or grownups?
- Now that you have a targeted group, what ages are they? For example, are you catering to individuals in their 20s or in their 50s?
- Where does your group live?
- What is the theme of your commercial?

Writing children's songs

If you are unfamiliar with writing children's songs, do your research. Visit record stores and ask for popular children's CDs and videos. Look also at children's programs that are usually aired on Saturdays. Also, look at television channels that are specifically geared towards children to get ideas.

Note also that children are quite aware of what is happening around them. Give them the words and melodies that they are familiar with. Remember you are writing for children of today. Therefore, do not compose songs with jargon that you were familiar with as a child as times have definitely changed.

Chapter 4: Working with Collaborators

One way to sharpen your songwriting skills is to work with a partner. Perhaps you have never done so before and you are a bit wary of doing so. Let us look at some of the successful collaborations in songwriting history.

Looking back in time, Mike Stoller and Jerry Leiber, were writers for Elvis Presley. Paul McCartney and John Lennon also worked together. They were members of the Beatles. There is also the collaboration between Elton John and Bernie Taupin.

If you work with a partner, these are some of the matters that should be taken into consideration:

Time

Perhaps you are a morning person and your brain is sharpest then whereas your partner's best time is late at night. Some form of compromise should be made and the best time to work, should be ascertained to avoid future conflicts.

Adhering to schedules

Perhaps you like to start on time but your partner always runs late. Choose someone who can commit.

Meet deadlines

Some people work best under pressure. If you are not one of them then you have to examine how you can do most of the work, way in advance before it gets to crunch time.

Ego

Though it is a collaboration, most times, egos can get in the way and personalities may clash. This is something you must acknowledge when selecting a partner.

Do not compete

Work with someone who does not see the work as a competition. This will hinder your progress.

Find different ways to constructively criticize

You do not have to blurt out that your partner's work sucks. You can simply encourage him or her to try writing from a different angle for example. Be more tactful as everyone has feelings.

Also, if you know you are overly sensitive, let your partner know how to inform you when he or she disapproves of something. Do not keep it bottled inside and then unleash your frustration inappropriately that it jeopardizes the partnership.

Learn to voice your opinions

There will be differences of opinions but you must determine when it is best to compromise and when it is best to put your foot down.

Determine the rules

Collaborating with someone doesn't mean that you cannot source other partners for different projects. Work out the best arrangement for you.

Finding the right partner

To find the right partner, you need to know yourself first and then determine what you are looking for. That way, you do not go through five partners in frustration when in reality you're the one who is at fault 99% of the time. If this occurs, you need to re-evaluate whether collaborating is best for you.

Are you looking for someone who is business oriented? Loyal? Someone who fits your personality? A nurturer? A great friend? Figure out ideally the personality traits that you prefer.

Scouting

Start looking for partners in your area. The songs that various bands perform that you like, find out who wrote them. Find out more about the songwriter. Get to know band members better as they can share valuable information.

Search the directory. Contact studios and producers in your area and ask questions. Set up meetings.

The next step, is to look at areas where the music industry is flourishes more. If your locale is a bit slow and boring but miles away, the music industry is booming and vibrant, explore that option. You may not have to relocate, but reach out to the experts in the field in that area. Social media is also a great way to find people and get the word out that you are looking for a partner.

Make sure that you have something to offer. You may have writer's block on a particular song but if thus far you have nothing to show, not the lines of any song or portfolio to engage others in conversation, then your chances will be slimmer. Take the time to organize your work and be prepared.

Entailed in this eBook are the names of great hits, singers, and songwriters in history. Perhaps you may view the information as insignificant. However, when you are discussing certain matters with others who are versed in the field, you will be glad that you have knowledge about certain matters. The world is your university. Not because you do not like a particular genre means that you should not know the basics about it.

You can also place advertisements in the newspapers and hand out flyers at certain events. Let people know what you are searching for, so the right people can apply. Be specific. Other areas you can place flyers are churches, music halls, and music stores.

Be more proactive in the field of networking.

The business standpoint

These are matters which must be determined from the onset.

- Who will own the copyright? Both of you?
- Percentage of royalties
- If the collaboration ends, and the song is not successful, can both of you ask someone to put a fresh spin on the song using material that the other person wrote?

One factor that can assist you with writing with more clarity, is minimizing stress. You can reduce stress by communicating with your partner and have rules and guidelines so that conflicts and arguments can be settled early.

Chapter 5: Use the Five Senses

Visual Power

There is an art in making your words come alive. Have you ever asked someone to tell you what a movie is about and when the individual is done, it is as if you've seen the movie? You may ask someone else and he or she struggles to find the right words.

Or perhaps, someone described a movie and in your excitement, as you have a wild imagination, you looked at it and you're absolutely stunned. It is nothing like how the person described it.

Improve your skill so that you do not fall in the latter category. Do not leave your listeners puzzled.

Has someone ever visited your neighborhood and he is talking about things that you take for granted? He raves over the restaurants, the scenic views, and even mentions your strange neighbors who are always arguing. These are things that you have numbed yourself to seeing or hearing.

Do not go through life with heavy shades on and your headphones very loud every waking hour that it makes you oblivious to what is around you. Be more aware. See things like a tourist or a child; in wonderment.

Start with your breakfast. Yes, it may sound silly but try it. As a songwriter, if you were asked to describe what you have eaten for breakfast or will have for breakfast, what will be your answer? Did you give a bland answer: toast and tea or cereal or waffles?

That's the answer, the average person gives. Be a little more creative. Pretend that you have a breakfast café and your life depends on persuading the public to dine at your café what would you convey? Come on in, we serve you toast and tea. What is so special about what you are serving compared to your competitors? Be more creative in your description.

As you go outside, what new sights have you overlooked for a long time? Change your route if everything looks the same. What is different with your new route when compared to your usual route? Why do you prefer your normal route? Why do you walk on a particular street to get to a place when there are other routes you can take? Has habit made you not open to appreciating other ways?

Perhaps you need to change your habits. See things differently. Sleep on the other side of the bed for a change and when you are sitting to have your breakfast, change your location. Pull a chair close to the window and enjoy breakfast. Change what you eat. Leave your home earlier or later if possible to see things differently. The exercise here is for you to see things from a different angle. It will open a new world up to you.

What books do you read? Do you have a particular genre that you prefer? What makes your favorite books so great? What do you like about them?

Have you ventured to read other genres? Does your favorite author write other genres? Have you tried one or are you sticking to what you have always read?

If you are not a reader, then you should. It opens an entirely different world up to you. It helps with your expressions and descriptions of characters and events.

If you have only listened to one type of music, explore other options. Listen to the legends in your genre.

Listen to instrumental music. If you had to put words to melodies what words would you choose?

Learn from your mistakes

It is wise not to dispose of your words, no matter how horrible they seem. Sometimes when you look at your writing pad, you may see so many crossing out that you can't even decipher the words you wrote. Why didn't the words work for you at the time? Can they be used if you had to write a different genre?

Revisit your work. In what way, would you currently describe what you previously wrote?

Examine the words to songs. How did the writer describe certain things?

Make the ordinary be more pronounced. For example, you are washing your car. As you wash your car what memories are flooding back to you? What great experiences have you had while driving your car? Was this the vehicle that you brought your first child home? Was this the vehicle that almost ran your neighbor's cat over? Unlock your memories.

Sound

Let us now examine sounds. We all know how sound effects can have us on the edge of our seats especially for horror movies. The actress is walking down a dark road and music intensifies your emotions. The actress walks faster and the music heightens even more. You may even put your hands over your eyes in fear of what is about to come.

When you are looking at a romantic movie, you surely won't hear metal music to evoke a tender scene.

Likewise, take notice of sounds on a daily basis. You may say that your area is quiet, but what does quiet mean? Absence of people yelling and cars screeching?

The world is never silent. Are there no birds in your area? They make a sound. Do you live close to the sea? Can you hear the waves crashing to the shore? Do you have pets or are there pets on your street? Are planes flying overhead? If it is nighttime, do you hear crickets chirping?

What sounds can you hear in your home? Is your faucet dripping? The fax machine making a sound? Is your refrigerator the noisy kind?

Infuse the sense of sound while writing. Even if you may not use the lines, do not limit yourself to just describing what you see or be selective in your hearing. Do not underestimate the power of sound.

Smell

I'm sure that you have countless experiences when you are feeling full, until you smell food and then all of a sudden you realize you are hungry. Or even if you are full, you will surely make room in your stomach if you are offered something very delicious.

How would you describe the various fragrances from flowers? Does a particular smell evoke certain memories? How can you inject a description of smell in your songs?

Taste

Do you watch shows where chefs whip up tasty treats and judges sample and critique accordingly? Imagine that you are one of those judges. Enjoy the food you eat. Sample food from different cultures. This exercise is about being more aware and being in the present moment.

Touch

When we think about touch, we more focus on the touching of another human. The softness of one's skin, texture of the hair, or fingertips running across someone's face.

Focus also on other things. Examine how it feels to touch, clothes, or sheets and other materials. When a spider or lizard runs across your feet how does it feel? Do you break out with goose bumps? How does it feel trying on a brand-new pair of comfortable shoes as oppose to one that is too tight?

This exercise is to make you more aware of things. When you are looking for a description find ways you can relate it to the five senses in a more creative way.

Look at the gestures people also make. Some people when nervous, play with their hair or become more animated. For example, perhaps you are describing when your significant other broke up with you. One of the memories you have is how before it happened, she or he kept playing with the ring that you gave as a gift. You noticed it but didn't understand the correlation until your significant other told you that he or she wanted to move on.

Colors

Have you ever reclined outdoors and sunlight hits your face? Sometimes you see colors. Colors have different meaning to people. Some colors evoke memories so also be mindful of how you can incorporate them.

Chapter 6: Starting With a Melody

How to write a melody?

You can pay a teacher to teach you to write a melody. Then, he will start playing or singing a new melody. But you know: **it will be teacher's melody, not yours**. You still won't know how it was created. Ok, the teacher can explain to you that a melody starts at some point, then goes up, then goes down, it moves through notes of one chord, and after, it moves through notes of the other chord. Then, the melody will reach some culmination point, and so on….

But, let me give you an example. Imagine that you are sitting at the table, and there is an apple on the table. There is also your teacher, who then tells you how to take this apple. He will start to explain to you that you must use some muscles of your arm to lift it and some other muscles to stretch it towards an apple. After that, you must use some other muscles to open your palm and then to grab an apple.

But it will be too complicated and too slow and will bring you great confusion. There is another way-**by trying**-and it could be much quicker.

You can choose one or two chords and start playing, humming, and searching for a melody. Then try to find the next chord and the next one-those best suited to your melody and to your own taste. The very first tip is to ensure that you do not rush over this task. It is extremely vital that you take your time and allow the inspiration to come.

Try to follow your intuition, listen to yourself, do not hurry, and wait until the feeling comes that this is the right tune. You are humming but do not try to push. I'm not saying this will work for anyone, but I know there are people who will succeed in such a way and who can master it. And it's a great feeling to write a song in this way.

I apply this method not only in songwriting, but also in improvising and playing solos on the guitar. It is the feeling when **you partially lead your improvisation, and it partially leads you**. Such an approach also helps to avoid clichés.

The process of creating a song shouldn't be forced by necessity. The relaxed state of mind and allowing your creativity to flow would give you much better results.

"Experience is the best teacher." - Late 16th; Tacitus

Writing a Song on Guitar

In order to write or compose a song on guitar, it is necessary to learn the **basic chords** first. Some beginners use the most common keys, which are G, D and C. As you learn the other keys, including the sharp keys, you will be able to explore and experiment in songwriting with a guitar.

If you already know the chords, keep on strumming until you create a good sound for the verse, chorus, and bridge. **Strum as if you are just playing** with different chords when you still do not have lyrics. You can try other song structures if you wish to sound unique from other compositions. It does not matter if you start making the melody first, before the lyrics, or the other way around.

Start humming the tune that you like and **sing the verse,** if possible, so you can check if it fits the chords. Play the melody, write the chords or tab it out. It is normal to have difficulty singing while playing during the first rehearsals, so if there is someone who can help you out and sing the song for you, then it would be nice.

People like to hear **unique sounds** and more catchy tunes. That is why you should avoid writing songs with the same keys and chords all the time. Find out which sound is perfect for the style of song that you wish to create. If you cannot avoid using the same keys over and over, then choose a different tempo and pitch to make it sound fresh and new.

Common Major Scale Chords in a Corresponding Key

KEY	I	II	III	IV	V	VI	*bVII
C	C	Dm	Em	F	G	Am	Bb
Db	Db	Ebm	Fm	Gb	Ab	Bbm	Cb
D	D	Em	F#m	G	A	Bm	C
Eb	Eb	Fm	Gm	Ab	Bb	Cm	Db
E	E	F#m	G#m	A	B	C#m	D
F	F	Gm	Am	Bb	C	Dm	Eb
Gb	Gb	Abm	Bbm	Cb	Db	Ebm	Fb
G	G	Am	Bm	C	D	Em	F
Ab	Ab	Bbm	Cm	Db	Eb	Fm	Gb
A	A	Bm	C#m	D	E	F#m	G
Bb	Bb	Cm	Dm	Eb	F	Gm	Ab
B	B	C#m	D#m	E	F#	G#m	A

* I added bVII degree, instead of VII, because it is widely used in pop/rock music. For example: **A Hard Day's Night by The Beatles** (G-C-G-F-G, I-IV-I- bVII-I), **All Right Now by Free** (chorus) (A-G-D-A, I- bVII-IV-I), **Crazy Little Thing Called Love by Queen** (D-G-C-G, I-IV-bVII-IV).

Common Minor Scale Chords in a Corresponding Key

KEY	I	III	IV	V	V	VI	VII
Cm	Cm	Eb	Fm	Gm	G, G7	Ab	Bb
C#m	C#m	E	F#m	G#m	G#, G#7	A	B
Dm	Dm	F	Gm	Am	A, A7	Bb	C
D#m	D#m	F#	G#m	A#m	A#, A#7	B	C#
Em	Em	G	Am	Bm	B, B7	C	D
Fm	Fm	Ab	Bbm	Cm	C, C7	Db	Eb
F#m	F#m	A	Bm	C#m	C#, C#7	D	E
Gm	Gm	Bb	Cm	Dm	D, D7	Eb	F
G#m	G#m	B	C#m	D#m	D#, D#7	E	F#
Am	Am	C	Dm	Em	E, E7	F	G
Bbm	Bbm	Db	Ebm	Fm	F, F7	Gb	Ab
Bm	Bm	D	Em	F#m	F#, F#7	G	A

Starting With a Chord Progression

If you have a talent to create interesting chord progressions on a keyboard or a guitar, start with them, play with them, and add some words, humming a melody. I think, most likely, the chord progression is not chosen before, but it comes during the process of songwriting. But if you feel like you don't have any good ideas, just come up with a good chord progression, and once you have it, hum a melody as you play the progression. This is going to give you a good start that you can use as a base.

You should also consider the kind of tune you are creating. If it evokes romantic feelings, you should create a song about love, but if it has an aggressive and upbeat sound, you should come up with energetic lyrics that might be about protest or raising awareness. When you have a nice chord progression, you can also try to create a simple solo over it.

Some of the Most Often Used Chord Progressions:

I - VI - IV - V	Song	Performed by
A F#m D E	Stand By Me	Ben E. King
F Dm Bb C	Complicated	Avril Lavigne
Db Bbm Gb Ab	Lucky (chorus)	Britney Spears
C Am F G	How Great is Our God (chorus)	Chris Tomlin
B G#m E F#	Wonderful World	Sam Cooke
Ab Fm Db Eb	Every Breath You Take	The Police
A F#m D E	I Will Always Love You	Whitney Houston

I - V - IV - V	Song	Performed by
Db Ab Gb Ab	Everything I Do	Bryan Adams
G D C D	Tangerine (chorus)	Led Zeppelin
D A G A	Under Pressure	Queen
A E D E	You Don't Know What Love Is	The White Stripes
C G F G	All The Small Things	Blink 182
Eb Bb Ab Bb	With You	Chris Brown

I VII VI	Song	Performed by
C# B A	Gimme Shelter	Rolling Stones
Cm Bb Ab	All Along the Watchtower	Jimi Hendrix
Am G F	outro section of Stairway to Heaven	Led Zeppelin
F#m E D	Under My Thumb	Rolling Stones

I - V - VI - IV	Song	Performed by
A E F#m D	Someone Like You (chorus)	Adele
A E F#m D	Already Gone	Kelly Clarkson
A E F#m D	The Edge Of Glory (chorus)	Lady Gaga
Ab Eb Fm Db	Paparazzi (chorus)	Lady Gaga
D A Bm G	Girlfriend (chorus)	Avril Lavigne
B F# G#m E	I'm Yours	Jason Mraz

VI - IV - I - V	Song	Performed by
Cm Ab Eb Bb	So Small	Carrie Underwood
Am F C G	Parachute	Cheryl Cole

Starting With a Guitar Riff

A memorable riff can make all the difference

We have all heard songs that are driven by their lyrical power, but there are also many compositions that shine because of their guitar riffs. A good example of a song that has a memorable riff is **Enter Sandman by Metallica** or **Smoke on the Water by Deep Purple**. The point is that a great riff can make a song shine, and the lyrics can be a perfect way to complement a great song structure.

Creating a good riff

A good riff is (not usually, but can be) the product of trial and error during a jam-session. This means, you might be playing some random ideas, and then something seems to click. Once you have an idea you like, you should start working on it and polishing it until you have a riff that you like. This is the way that most great riffs are made. Going back to the **Enter Sandman** example, the band tells a story about how the original riff was created by Kirk, but if it wasn't for the tweaks that Lars added to it, the riff would probably not have been as good, or maybe it could have been even better if they left it as it was.

The important thing to take out of that little story about how that riff was made is that you will usually modify a riff at least a little. That is not to say that some riffs have not been composed in a sudden creative moment and have been left exactly as they first came out. Such is the case with **Megadeth's Symphony of Destruction** main riff.

How do you write a song around a riff?

I think it is relatively easy for guitarists to create a good riff, but the main problem for many musicians could be this: ***What`s next? How do you write a song around a riff?*** That's why **I tried to analyze** some of excellent songs with good riffs.

Some guitar riff application types could be:

The song starts with a great, memorable riff

The song starts with a great riff then the 1st verse follows at the same key as the riff. Melody is very static, simple, monotonous, and sometimes, improvising (the singer improvises a melody), based on one, maybe 2 chords.

Examples:

Deep Purple - Smoke on the Water (verse-2chords G and F),

The Rolling Stones - (I Can't Get No) Satisfaction (verse – 2chords E, A),

Black Sabbath - Paranoid,

Nirvana - Smells Like Teen Spirit.

Riff based songs (the riff continuous during the verse)

Examples:

Cream - Sunshine of Your Love,

Led Zeppelin - Whole Lotta Love,

Red Hot Chili Peppers - Can't stop,

Blur - Song 2,

David Bowie - Rebel Rebel (2 chords D and E),

Muse - Supermassive Black Hole (verse-1 chord E),

The White Stripes - Seven Nation Army,

Dire Straits - Money for Nothing,

AC/DC - Back in Black,

The Beatles - I Feel Fine,

Megadeth - Symphony of Destruction.

You can see in the song, **Can't Stop by Red Hot Chili Peppers,** the riff is continuous during the first verse, and the melody is very monotonous, but the chorus is contrasting, melodic.

Riffs based on blues progressions

Examples:

Chuck Berry - Johnny B Goode,

The Kinks - You Really Got Me,

The Beatles -I Feel Fine,

Good Golly Miss Molly-performed by CCR.

Riffs followed by melodic verse

Examples:

Pretty Woman – Roy Orbison

If you have a good riff that is very catchy, then my suggestion would be - the melody of the 1st verse after that riff should be very static with one, maybe 2 chords, not more.

Writing a song on guitar should always be an experience that understands the structure of a good song, but is not afraid of exploring ideas. This is going to be the most honest way for anyone to create music. Always follow your instincts and think about how good a song really sounds to you. ***Is the chorus catchy, and are the riffs really good, or just OK?*** These are the kinds of questions you need to ask yourself when writing a song on guitar.

How to Write Song Lyrics

When it comes to writing melodies and the structure for songs, many musicians have little difficulty expressing the music side of their talent. However, when it comes to how to write song lyrics, it can seemingly be a different matter. In fact, there are many musicians who believe that the art of songwriting cannot be taught, but instead, the person must have that talent already inside them.

This is because the personal expression of music and the lyrics come from two different parts of the brain that must be united in order to create a song. While some may say it takes talent that is already present, there are too many people who have demonstrated the ability to learn how to write lyrics over the years. So, it is not so much inherited talent as understanding how to merge the melody with the words and create a good, solid song.

Where Do Song Lyrics Come From?

There is no end to the sources from where song lyrics may come, but for the most part, they do evolve out of the experiences of the person who is writing the music. Quite often, this is combined with their emotions, feelings, and beliefs that find expression along with the melody. While seemingly profound in concept, some of the most famous song lyrics actually have rather humble origins.

For example, the **Dire Straits'** classic **"Skateaway"** sprang from a taxi cab ride that band leader, **Mark Knopfler**, was taking in London, when he spotted a girl skating down the sidewalk in brightly colored clothing and wearing a brand-new Sony Walkman radio. The image that **Knopfler** had was so strong that he constructed the entire melody and lyrics out of the five or ten seconds that he observed the girl.

When it comes to your lyrics, finding the right ones will often come from some type of experience you had, even if it was only dreamed or perhaps imagined. The key is finding the right way to incorporate them into the song itself.

How to Incorporate Lyrics into Songs

So, when you have created the perfect melody, how can you write song lyrics that compliment what you have accomplished? Quite often, the answer does not spring to mind, although there have been exceptions. **Robert Plant** wrote the lyrics to **"Stairway to Heaven"** in just a few minutes, as the inspiration came to him rather quickly.

Unfortunately, the rule, generally, is that you will have to work a little harder than Robert did on that particular song in order to come up with some good lyrics. However, you can emulate what **Robert Plant, Mark Knopfler**, and many other songwriters have done, trying to meld the feelings that you have into words that add to the melody. The only important result is the final one, where you understand what you want out of the words you create for the song.

Hooks: You may have created melodic hooks to your song, but lyrics can provide hooks as well. There are many examples where a certain phrase becomes a hook in the song that compliments the melody and creates a more memorable result in totality. A real plus to creating lyrical hooks is they do not need to be sophisticated to be memorable.

Cher's "Believe" was auto-tuned in certain parts to create a very memorable effect. You can also cite the **Gnarls Barkley** classic, **"Crazy"**, as a song that took a very common word, in fact a word that worked for Patsy Cline's version over a half century ago, and gave it a new meaning. Creating hooks with lyrics is nothing new, but it is something that works out quite well.

Percussive: Another way you can write lyrics for a song is by incorporating the percussive nature of the words themselves. Many rap and hip hop songs use this technique, but it can be used for many different genres. **The Psychedelic Furs**, for example, wrote a song called **"Pulse"** for their first album, which used the words as percussive instruments, where the sound was more important than the meaning of the words themselves.

Message: This may be the most common way to provide a hook for your lyrics in that they convey a message that the audience will understand. This is true, even if the lyrics make no sense. For example, when asked by the producer of their first feature film to write a title song, **Paul McCartney** and **John Lennon** managed to write, **"A Hard Day's Night"** all in one night, built around a throwaway line that **Ringo Starr** had said a few months earlier.

Sourcing Your Lyrics

Whether you choose to create lyrics with hooks, messages, or as percussive instruments, you will need to find the inspiration necessary to create them. The good news is, when it comes to learning how to write song lyrics, the inspiration can come from anywhere. From books, television shows, the radio, the internet, watching people walk across the street or listening to someone say how tough their night was by proclaiming they had to work all day.

It helps if you can combine the feeling the melody gives you with an experience that you had or something you have seen or heard. Quite often, lyrics have inspirations that come from the most unlikely sources, but you have to be aware of the moment when it strikes. This means having a pen and paper handy or perhaps a smartphone in which you can quickly type a message to yourself when the lyrics start to flow.

The initial stages are the most important, as you can then work off of your inspiration and come up with additional lyrics based on your original idea. Of course, you might find that your lyrics will change radically over time, but that is okay, as long as you start the creative process. After all, there is no one way to learn how to write song lyrics, but you can find yourself tapping into a source that provides what is needed to complete the song itself.

Starting With a Title

Some songwriters start their music with a title. The title will be the general topic and their basis for the lines used in the verses and chorus. These songwriters consider the title very important in every aspect of song composition, because all the ideas may come from it. They can list several titles to choose from or simply make a final title in a snap. However, other musicians can just decide about the title afterwards, since they can base it from the lyrics.

The title should be **catchy and easy to remember**. Shorter titles have greater impact, but sometimes meaningful or intriguing, long phrase titles are interesting too. Some musicians do not use direct or clear titles; they use hidden meanings to make the song look mysterious.

It's not for my taste to start a song with a title, but as I mentioned earlier, there is no right or wrong way. You can choose an interesting, catchy title and then build a song around it. **One of the simplest methods is to answer the questions.**

For example:

1) I Can't Forgive Her.

Ask the questions! Why? When did it start? Where did it start? What will be next? What is important to you? What is important to her? Do you know her well? Does she know you? Do you trust her? What should I do? Must I forgive or not? And so on…

2) Millions of Stars.

Which of them is yours? Which is mine? How did they arise? When did they arise? How long will they shine? What will happen with them? What will happen with us? What will happen with our feelings?

3) My friend.

What is my friend like? Will he ever gossip about me? Will he be able to forgive? Will he believe me when any other will not? Is love a choice or a feeling?

4) Step By Step

Do we run? Do we walk? Do we drive? Do we float along with stream of life? What is our direction? What are our goals? What can stop us? Are we directed by fear or by the call of our heart?

Writing a Song If You Don't Play Any Instrument

It is not impossible to write songs, even if you cannot play any musical instrument. Some people have the talent to write lyrics or make a melody even if they cannot read notes or understand chords; these people find themselves **humming** or **whistling** a tune and automatically create a catchy song.

Knowledge in any musical instrument is definitely an advantage for musicians and composers. Nowadays, modern gadgets and apps are available to help any aspiring musician to write or compose a song without playing an instrument.

The most recommended tool in writing a song is the **pre-recorded music tracks** that you can buy from specific websites. There are free options for those who prefer more practical recording. These song tracks are not limited to one genre and are available with a full band setup if needed.

Some websites allow users to record voice, and they **add back up instruments or beats** for free, but if you want to convert the song into MP3 file format, then you have to pay for it, albeit a minimum fee. These websites are fun to use and can give an idea on what tunes and style to use in your composition.

Some aspiring musicians, who cannot play any musical instrument, may not feel comfortable using online recording apps. The best way is to record it just like the **old way**. Get a voice recorder or use your mobile phone recorder then hum the tune if lyrics are not yet available.

When you're done with the melody, lyrics, and song structure, maybe you can **hire someone** to plot your song to chords or tabs. When you have chords and notes, it is easier to ask someone, like another musician or a band mate, to play your song, since they can follow the exact tones that you have created.

When you are planning to write a song, you may want to listen to great artists and musicians first. Listen to the **melody** and **lyrics** then study the possible **structures**. Some songs have long introductions, either instrumental or with lyrics. Check how verses were written; these are important, since these are where the stories are told.

Problems

One of the problems or, rather, features of songwriting can be that while the song is being written, **you do not see it as a whole**. You only see the beginning or the part of the song on which you are working. It is like walking in darkness without seeing where to go.

You may feel that a part on which you are working is still not good, and you modify it; you change it, even though, in the context of the song, it would be good. One of the main mistakes is to try to put **too much** material and ingenuity in the first verse and try to create it to be very impressive. And then there is no longer space for further development and contrasts.

Imagine you walk along one of New York's streets in rush hour, and people are coming towards you, rushing past you, crossing your path. But you continue moving forward, although you can't predict everything in your path trajectory. You do not wait until the street becomes empty, and you will be able to see all your way.

Similarly, when you are composing a song, do not sit at one of its parts, constantly trying to improve it. Go ahead with other parts, and when your song's structure becomes mainly clear, then you can go back and change and improve it.

Writer's Block

I think it is very individual, and everybody has his own approach, but personally, I sometimes feel inspired when I hear a bad song. I have the desire then to write something much better.

The flow of words from brain to paper is a consistently regular task for writers all over the world, and this firmly includes songwriters. However, as you keep writing, there comes that disruptive element that seems to make you feel like you can't go any further, and you need to stop. Now, it's vital to know that it's actually all happening in your mind, when it seems like you can't go further, and you can't think of anything else. Therefore, there are quite a number of ways for songwriters to overcome the song writing block.

The very first thing you need to do is **take a break**. This is the time when you should just walk away and relieve yourself of some of the labour that comes with writing. The important thing to note is that the human brain will always need rest at some point, and due to the level of creativity involved in writing, it is only right that you should give your brain some rest.

If you want to get more tips on writer's block, you can download my FREE report, "15 Tips to Overcome Songwriter's Block", at my site: yoursongwriting.com.

How to Freestyle Rap

I'm not a rap freestyle specialist, but the reason I mentioned it in my book is that, in my opinion, for every songwriter, no matter what style he writes, it would be useful to learn to freestyle rap, because it can improve his lyrics writing skills and elevate them to a new level, as well as improve the ability to improvise.

If you want to learn different techniques, you may listen to other professional rappers who have made albums, singles, or are even known for **freestyle rapping battles**. You may find videos of international artists on the internet and listen to how they deliver the words and notice the rhymes at the end of each line.

There are so many American rappers, who can inspire anyone who wishes to learn the skill in freestyle rapping, such as the late Tupac Shakur and Notorious B.I.G or Eminem. They are known for rap songs with deep meaning. Eminem is more famous for freestyle rapping, since he started joining street battles before he became famous.

Just like any other rapper, you must **listen carefully to the beat** and try to understand the counts in order to fill in the appropriate number of words and syllables. Since you are just a beginner, you may write down your rap lyrics first then look for a simple and average tempo beat on some websites such as **YouTube**.

There are available **videos** with instrumental music or beats, especially made for rappers and enthusiasts, by some DJs. If you have a keyboard instrument at home, you can use the available beats there and adjust the tempo to whatever speed you prefer. Another option is to get a karaoke version of your favorite rap songs and try to compose your own lyrics on the spot.

Do not be disappointed if you cannot follow the beat or cannot think of rhyming words at times, because that happens to everyone, especially to beginners, and that is the reason you have to rehearse often.

Practice **improvising lyrics**. Think of a specific subject, such as Love, War, or Freedom, and think of how you want to describe the topic. Let your mind flow freely and do not force yourself to concentrate on a specific idea.

It is also advisable to **write down rhymes** to the words that you commonly use on your rap pieces. By this, you can create sentences or lines more easily. If you want to focus, you must rehearse in a private area, so you will not be distracted by any other sound, aside from the beat that you are following.

Freestyle rapping includes **fillers**. It is possible for rappers, even the professional ones, to forget the next line or go blank for seconds. The best way to avoid these moments is to use fillers or filler words and phrases, such as yeah, come on, that's right, yo, yes, here it goes. The purpose of fillers is to keep the freestyle rap from falling apart, so it should not be overused, or else, you will end up with a non-sense and boring rap song.

You can be creative and choose funny words or lines, catchy statements and similes, or start your rap lyrics with a shocking intro, but not necessarily something explicit. It is important to feel confident and let your ideas flow and to play with words, as long as it makes a lot of sense and is entertaining.

Some Songwriting Tips

A good song can be created by anyone, even those who may have little to no formal musical training. This is because everyone has an inherent musical ability, and writing a good song does not need tremendous talent to make it happen. However, it does require a little thought, discipline, and ability to translate what is in your head to the page, so your song can become a reality.

Fortunately, there are methods that can make this happen, which songwriters have been using for many decades. By following these tips, you can understand how to make a song a reality.

Tap into Your Emotions

A good song stirs your emotions, so it's no surprise that songwriters will tap into their emotions when writing a song and, in particular, the lyrics. You'll want the lyrics to reflect a real passion and intensity that brings out an emotional response. When you believe in the lyrics, they take on a whole new life that will help elevate the entire song.

Listen to Your Passions

Successful songwriters have an ability to tap into their passions, which then translate into good songwriting material. This is because the really good songs are the ones that relate to the emotion, drive, and interest of the songwriter. There are many different things that people are passionate about: love, money, family, and more. Some songs revolve around the loss of youth or days gone by, while others look forward into the future. Whatever fuels your passions should be the source of your songwriting.

Write Down Ideas Immediately

When you think of a great lyric or song idea, write it down on the spot and don't try to put it off. Carry a pad and pen or pencil with you, so when an idea pops into your head, you can put it straight to paper. In this manner, you can retain more of your lyric ideas and create more songs.

Take a Walk

Unfortunately, song ideas generally do not come from the ether as you sit in your comfortable chair. For the most part, they have to be inspired during some activity. One good way to help stir up some song ideas is by taking a walk in the country. A good hike in the fresh air will help the blood flow to your brain, which in turn, helps bring out more inspiration. In fact, getting out of the house and doing any number of healthy activities is a great way to stir the imagination and bring out great song ideas. So, whether you go for a walk, ride a bike, or take your travels to other parts of the world, your inspiration is out there.

Turn the Bad into the Good

For whatever reason, more people will remember the bad experiences in their lives over the good, even if they do not talk about them as much. The good news is that the bad experiences make for great songwriting material, as some of the most unforgettable songs have been about experiences that didn't quite go the way the songwriter wanted. As inspirational works, you can tap into your bad experiences in life and turn them into songs that do not have to be sad. In fact, they can be funny and even uplifting.

Work With Others

Sometimes, the best way to make a song is to find someone else to collaborate. You don't have to go any further than **Paul McCartney** and **John Lennon** to see what a collaborative effort means to creating songs. And while your songs may not become as popular as **The Beatles'**, you can still get a great deal of inspiration and joy from working with others while collaborating on songs. Quite often, collaboration is one person coming up with song ideas, while the other makes a few changes or edits to improve the overall effect.

Try Reading

By taking the time to read newspaper headlines, stories, magazines, blogs, and many different text sources, you can come up with great inspiration for your songs. Not only will you be provided with good song material, you will also expand your vocabulary, which you can use when writing lyrics. Reading should be part of your everyday activities.

Be Random

One of the best ways to choose song lyrics is by coming up with a few sayings or sentences along with your friends and pulling them out of a hat. You can even write just a word or two on each note and then pull two or three to make a sentence or simply an idea. Try singing the lyrics that you pull out of the hat, and if they work, you can try to put them into a song. It may sound really random at first, but when you think about how many great songs have lyrics that seem random, such as **"Burning Down the House"** by the **Talking Heads**, this method can really work.

Chapter 7: Chords, Keys, and Progressions

In order to write songs, a little knowledge of music theory is necessary. If you want to write and communicate your musical ideas to others, then you need to know how things like key signatures, chord progressions, scales and the other basic concepts of music function. In this chapter, we are going to take a very simple look at the elements of music theory that are helpful for a songwriter to know. If you are serious about learning to write music, you'll want to do some reading up on music theory. It will help you be a better player, teacher, writer and also increase your employment options, should you want to make a career as a musician.

The Note

We're going start our discussion of music theory with the "note". A note is a single sound. Western music has named twelve notes and they are are arranged in different ways to make a bunch of different kinds of scales.

A scale is a group of notes, played in a certain pattern, the most common of which is called the "Major Scale." The major scale is what people are singing when you hear them sing "Do Re Mi Fa So La Ti So".

We're going to skip over how we get major scales because it isn't that important to the topic of writing songs and get write to chords.

The Chord

A chord is more than one note, arranged in a pattern that are played at the same time. It's a group of a few notes that sound good when played together. Notes are like letters, and chords are like words. In Western music, chords are comprised of at least three different notes. They can have notes, but never less.

Each major scale makes its own set of chords. How this happens is a little more complicated than we need to get right now. What you need to know is that each major scale makes a group of chords that all sound good together. It's like a kit that contains everything you need to write songs. These "Kits" are called "Keys."

Let's take a look at C major scale. The absence of altered notes makes the C major scale and the chords we can construct from it perfect for exploring music theory without getting too bogged down. We'll discuss other keys briefly before we are done.

The notes in a C major scale are: C D E F G A B C.

Scales always start and end on the same note. Each one of the notes in the C Major scale can be turned into a chord, there are seven different notes in a scale so we can get seven different chords. Don't worry how we got the chords for now. The chords we get from the C major scale are:

Chord Progressions

A chord progression is the order in which the chords change, or the order that you play them in. To make things simpler to write down, Roman numerals are used instead of the chord's name. Major Chords get upper case (I, IV, V), and minor chords get lower case (ii, iii, vi) and diminished chords are lower case with usually a circle or asterisk after them (vii*).

That's all the theory you need to know to get through the exercises in this book and to start writing your own songs. If you found this chapter a little confusing, it will make sense after a few re-readings. Just remember that there are twelve "Keys". Each Key contains a bunch of tools to write songs with. It has chords and scales that already go well with each other. There are seven different chords in every key, and the most important ones are the I, IV and V. In the key of C, these chords are C major, F major and G major.

Playing With Chord Progressions

As far as the theory stuff goes, knowing about keys and how chords relate to each other is vital to songwriting. We talked a little about chord progressions using the Roman numerals, but now let's take a more practical look at them.

The seven chords in the key of C all get along well with each other. You can randomly select two chords and switching between them will sound pretty good. That's why people write songs in keys- everything you need is already there. Over time, some progressions have become well known and common. That's OK, don't be afraid to use them. Grab your instrument and try these progressions:

I-IV C Major- F Major

IV-I F Major - C Major

I-vi C Major - A Minor

I-iii C Major - E Minor

iii-vi E Minor - A Minor

I-IV-V C Major - F Major - G Major

V-I-IV-I G Major - C Major - F Major - C Major

I-vi-IV-V C Major - A Minor - F Major - G Major

So far we have looked at how chords are derived from scales and how they are strung together to produce chord progressions. What we haven't talked about it how long each chord is to be played - how many beats or measures each cord is supposed to last before changing to another chord. Right now it is better for you to just play with the progressions and not worry about the rhythmic end of the pool. You probably already know the basics of rhythm and how to count out bars or measures of music.

If all of this talk of chords, progressions, and Roman numerals is getting to you, that's perfectly normal. Music theory is a bit weird to understand when you are new to it. There're lots of rules; new symbols to learn and it seems like it contradicts itself at every twist and turn. The truth is that it does contradict itself, sort of, and it is definitely confusing. Music Theory operates according to a self-contained logic. It makes sense within itself. There's also a lot to it. Don't expect it to be clear to you for weeks. Just keep at it and soon enough you'll begin to understand. It's important to know that the rules of music theory are rules, in the commonly understood sense. They are just suggestions about what sounds good. A IV always likes to move to the I chord and will always sound good, no matter the style or age of music. It doesn't mean you HAVE to follow every IV chord with a I chord, just that if you do, it'll sound good. Knowing these rules helps you when you are stuck on a song and don't know where to go.

Let's take a break from the theory and look at some ways to effectively encourage and capture inspiration. We'll get back into it a little more in a bit.

Chapter 8: Dealing With Inspiration

Capturing Inspiration

Ben Franklin recommended that everyone carry around a little notebook and record their ideas on it as they have them. He claimed that this single habit was responsible for all of his success in life. This is great advice not only for inventors but for every creative person. Luckily, these days the songwriter has something much better - the smartphone. We brought this up in previous chapter, but it's worth talking more about.

Twenty years ago it would take a small room full of thousands of dollars of gear to duplicate all the ways a smartphone can help you write songs. Using nothing more than your phone and a few inexpensive apps, it is now possible to type lyrics, make voice notes of ideas or melodies and record complete demo songs anywhere and anytime.

This ability to quickly capture ideas and organize them for later use is a great thing to be able to do, to be able to accomplish all of this with a single device that fits in your pocket is nothing short of amazing. There's no excuse for not taking Ben's advice, and once you realize the difference it makes in your creative output, you won't want to stop.

Capturing inspiration is often likened to putting lighting in a bottle, that is to say, it's impossible to do and foolish to try. This isn't really the case, though, dealing with and channeling inspiration requires discipline and practice. If you're not willing to work at it, you won't have much success.

The first step is to get in the habit of recording or writing down every idea for a song that you have. Don't trick yourself into thinking you'll remember it later. Just make a quick voice note or jot down a few words. After a few weeks, you should have a nice pile of ideas that will help you get started on a few tunes. Don't judge your thoughts, just record them. You never know when that stupid lyric you wrote months ago will fit perfectly with that new line you wrote in the elevator this morning. This is how many songs get written- a little bit here, a little bit there.

As making notes becomes a habit, you'll find that when you sit down to play or write, you're more focused, and things will "flow" more easily. This is because you're in a constant state of "priming the pump" all day as you're mulling over your ideas and on the lookout for new ones.

Another practice that helps the process of encouraging inspiration is regular writing sessions. Writing songs, even when you feel like you have no ideas or anything interesting to say, is an important part of becoming proficient at the process. Set aside a few nights a week to spend an hour or so just writing or working on songs.

Try giving yourself a challenge such as "I'm going to write a blues song about a guy who won the lotto." and write it.

Don't worry about whether or not it is any good- just write a song. Even if you throw it in the trash and never mention it again- it's still a song. Inspiration won't visit every time you sit to write, but it will come around a lot more often if you give it a space in your life. If you dutifully record your ideas and discipline yourself to work consistently, it won't be long before you have a nice collection of homegrown tunes and a good understanding of your creative process.

Taking advantage of inspiration involves quite a bit of discipline and consistency. The more you try, the easier it gets. Make a promise to yourself to start jotting down those ideas now, before you lose any more songs!

Encouraging Inspiration

While there is no way that I know of to turn on and off creative inspiration like a light switch, there are some things that seem to make it easier to come by. For one, make sure you are listening to, reading, and watching things that challenge how you think and stir up your emotions. Pay attention to the types of art that move you. Ask yourself what is it, exactly, that makes it something meaningful to you?

Inspiration can be hiding everywhere. If you want, it to. Hank Williams Sr, the country music legend, once said that romance comic books gave him many song ideas. Sound silly? Who cares! Hank found something that worked and went with it. Lots of silly, potentially embarrassing things can provide you with song ideas- don't close yourself off to anything. The subject matter for your songs should come from more than just your personal experiences. Other people's stories and experiences are also good sources of ideas, so is fiction. Keep your eyes open.

It's a bad idea to put limits on what can and cannot inspire you. Part of being inspired is encountering the new and unfamiliar, as long as you have your smartphone or tiny notebook, you'll never miss out on these wonderful moments again. Be shamelessly nonjudgmental about your ideas until the proper time. When you are just making notes or sketching out a new song for the first time, don't worry about the quality. Just enjoy the process.

Chapter 9: Singing with Syllables, a Way to Find Your Rhythm

As a songwriter, you must have gone through these phases where you have melodies coming to you, out of nowhere, or again, you might sometimes wake up singing a phrase out of nowhere, over and over. As an artist, this could be assimilated to your genius being at work, or again to your creativity being stimulated. For those who are wondering as to how this creativity is being stimulated, well, anything can trigger it, like a song on TV, or a scene involving people that you may have noticed after taking a walk outside. Our point is that as a songwriter or an aspiring songwriter, you should have this ability to have your sense of creativity being triggered just about anywhere and anytime. So, take a listen to these sounds or musical "vibes" visiting you from time to time. With that being said, let us start with our first step to writing a great song in only a day.

-Mentally Capture the Sang Melody of your song

One thing is certain you don't necessarily have the lyrics to your song come to you as easy as you wished, but amazingly, melodies are easily assimilated and imagined. Most singers or aspiring artists probably know what I am talking about here. It is this fragment of a melody (or a simple sentence) that becomes obsessive the more you hear it. Amazingly enough, the more you "hum" or play this melody in your head, the more the rest of the song reveals itself (we're talking about a melody here, not lyrics).

Do you get what I am talking about? So, technically you already have the inspiration source there, but the big problem lies with being faithful to that original sound, but you will see throughout the book how this can be achieved, and a bit easier than you think.

First, you have to capture this piece of melody (as it is always a fragment of a song that normally plays in the artist's mind), by making sure your mind records it (because it often happens that even the brightest artists forget an idea that seemed to be fresh and accessible because it was in their mind). One way to really materialize this piece of melody is by first humming it. You will not only hum it (making the "hum" sound), but you will try to "capture" it by methodically closing your eyes while you are doing it and use your finger to guide you through the process, and this is why:

-Closing your eyes, helps you keep distractions away and perform this task effectively. You can be alone in a room trying to write a song, but still be thinking about something else (being distracted), which might steal some time to the writing task, in the end. So, close your eyes throughout the first writing step.

-The use of a finger, helps you stay on track, because you not only have more focus, but you are also measuring "the flow" or intensity of the song. Let's explain. By using your finger, you are in a sort replicating your voice and measuring the long notes (remember you still don't have the lyrics, so you are still humming the song), and giving you an indication of how long a certain verse (or sang melody because you still don't have any lyrics) will be, and how high a note (or notes) should be.

This preliminary step, also helps you use your ears, where sounds slowly transform into syllables with distinctive sounds in the end, like "e", "m", "o" or a long "oooh" or "aaa", etc (whatever your preferred singing technique is).

This step should last 30 minutes (if you can time it, it's up to you), this way you can optimize efficacy (because your creativity is triggered) and don't lose patience.

-Sing the Melody with Syllables:

Once you have completed the first stage of your writing, proceed to mimic the melody by singing with syllables. This process should last between 40 minutes to an hour because it is very repetitive, and it helps you get comfortable and confident with the melody so that you can carry on with the next phase.

This is how you should proceed here:

-Take each sound, which makes up the fragment of the melody that has inspired you to write the song in the beginning, and divide them into different segments, each representing a syllable, like for instance:

"Dah, dah, daaaah!" This first line is supposed to represent a very distinct portion of your melody, which could be the first verse. You can see that these are simple syllables, that can be stretched (like daaah), to show how flexible singing syllables can be.

-To show a little difference between the tones or inflections, you can also differentiate syllables, like "do" for sadder or shorter notes and "e" for inflections (you know like the sounds Whitney Houston and Mariah Carey make in order to personalize their songs).

-Repeat the sounds orally, twice.

-Then, write down the syllables, while you repeat them a third time.

-Carry on by proceeding the same way with the rest of your melody (remember that so far, we've been working with a fragment of your melody), and sing with syllables like you've done so far.

-Your last step would be to record the sang syllables. Make sure you complete this task by respecting the type of speed you would like to keep, as this will help you evaluate the number of words you'd like each verse to have when you start writing down the lyrics (in later stages).

- What you will have to remember about this chapter is that:

- One, you need to capture the melody of the song first by learning to sing it with syllables.

- Use the sound "aaa", "o", or long sounds like "Ooooooh" depending on whether you are writing a love song, a song with a strong message or a more rhythmic song.

- Keep your eyes shut during the whole session, letting your finger guide your voice.
- End your session by recording the whole process and keep this as your first arrangement, which will be used for your writing in later stages.

Let's now move on to the next phase of your writing.

Chapter 10: Add Some Background Voices

To carry on with your writing in the most productive way, especially when you'll have to perform this task in just one day, you will have to add in some activities that will push your imagination even further (here we are still talking about creativity). One way to achieve this is by anticipating background singers. The reason why imagining background voices is important is because they help you find your rhythm, your keynotes (or tone) and, above all, the right wording.

So, how do you proceed here? First, think of the type of song you would like to write. If it's a ballad you wish to write, imagine background sounds such as a soft "hum" sounds. If it's a song aimed at making people dance, imagine background sounds made up of high notes like very high and long "Aaaaah" sounds, almost deafening, which will be a bit faster than the ones used for a ballad. Finally, if your song is aimed at grasping people's attention with a strong message, think about background sounds (again, representing background singers), imagine a very sharp but distinct "o" sound (think of a judge making a very firm final judgment and how serious this judge is constrained to appear).

This step in your writing will help you come up with a theme faster (set up a tone by taking into consideration the type of song you wish to write).

The next step would be to play your initial melody, by slowly inserting the background vocals by proceeding the following way:

-First, close your eyes and mimic the background voices you have chosen (either the "hum" sounds for a ballad, the "Aaaah" sounds for a more rhythmic song and finally a firm "o" for a song with a strong message.)

-Replay these sounds (always by mimicking them) one more time and make sure you harmonize the melody by adding as many background voices as possible (it could be one, two, three or more voices).

-Next, start inserting your initial melody. This is done by playing the background vocals through your head (with your eyes still closed) and mimicking your initial melody that we've discussed in previous chapter. Don't rush this step, take your time so that you really coordinate the background voices and yours, all in syllables (do not forget that we have not written any lyric yet).

-Repeat this process three more times, by keeping your focus making sure there are no noises, no disruptions, but only you, with your eyes shut, mimicking the background voices to your song and your own voice, the whole thing in syllables.

-After the third time, start writing down whatever word comes to your mind. Again, do not rush and let your mind work by letting the ideas flow from your brain to the piece of paper where you are writing your draft. When ideas stop coming out, stop the whole process. Do not force anything because you will get your change to adjust the wording, later on, today.

-Now, try and sing in the words you've just written and see how it works with this small piece of melody which will inspire your whole song, later on.

After you are done with this process, you should have your first set of keywords to your song matching your melody and background vocals. This whole new combination will now give you a better idea for a theme to your song.

This whole process should not take over 3 hours, but everyone is different, so, some people might work faster or take a bit longer. All that matters is that you come up with your first set of keywords.

- What you should remember about this stage is that:

- Adding background voices triggers your imagination even more.

- There are different types of background voices, depending on the type of song you wish to write.

- This technique will not only help you come up with your first set of words also known as keywords, but also give you a glimpse of what the theme of your song will end up being, in the end.

You can now move on to the next phase of your writing, which involves a step further into your final song on a very short delay.

Chapter 11: Add Some Movements to the Process

There is one more step you need to achieve before you proceed with the actual writing of your song, which is to add some movements to your initial arrangement, so you can fit the right number of words in a verse and in your chorus. Does that make sense to you?

Let's now proceed. First, avoid any type of distraction, like any outside noise, but also during the whole process. In other words, your movement or rhythm should consist of "deaf sounds" or sounds that are not distracting, such as tapping on your lap or tapping your foot on the floor. You will do so in order to achieve a more enjoyable phase of the writing process, where you will truly get into the mood of the song, which will also speed up the wording process (where more keywords will come out with more ease, taking you closer to the theme of your song). So, first, tap of your lap by counting to four (like 1, 2, 3, 4). If it's a ballad you will count slowly, if it's a more rhythmic song you will count faster and if it's a song aimed at sensitizing people you will count moderately (not too fast, not too slow).

Next, start singing in syllables like you have learned to do in previous chapters, but high enough, as if you were singing in front of a large crowd. Repeat this process at least five times (it could be more), and the more you'll progress the more you'll see your melody evolve in terms of how you embody it (where your feel like you are "owning the song" now), and where what used to be a series of simple sounds like "Aaaah", "o" or "oooh" now become real words. You will notice that these words will mostly come out of nowhere and that they naturally emerge because in your mind, they sound right, like, for instance, the sound "Aaaah!" can easily become "togetheeeeer", or "ooooh!" can easily change into "I love you". Or again, there might be an inflection appearing here and there (you know these little pleasant sounds that make a song so unique and pleasant).

As you come up with more words start writing them down. At this point, anything is important and an asset to your final song. The words appearing at this stage of your writing will, for the most part, sound right, they can also be considered as keywords and you might find them difficult to replace, so they should also be considered for your final draft.

Use each one of these new words and insert them into your melody and the words you've previously found. Then, do the following:

-Tap your lap or tap your foot on the floor, and "hum" the little arrangement you've come up with, so far (your melody added to a rhythm (1,2,3,4 either slow, fast or moderate) added to your keywords and some syllables (because you haven't got all the wording put up together yet).

-Make it a free singing session, where you let your emotions flow into the song. This will help you add some flavor or color to the song and make it easy for you to adopt a theme to it.

The whole process will mostly last 2 hours (it is an approximation, it could go beyond that).

- What you must retain from this chapter is that:

- One, movements such as tapping on your lap or foot give you a clear indication of how long a line in a verse should be.

- Movements help you stay on track with the timing.

- With movements, you know how to sing a line or a note.

- It helps you complete your list of keywords.

- It helps you get into the song and triggers your creativity even more.

This stage will make you excited enough about the song and help you move on to the next phase of your writing.

CHAPTER 12: AVOID THE TURN-OFFS

I've heard a few people say that songwriters are the craziest bunch of people they have had to work with among all creative types in the music business. I would tend to agree with that statement. Actually, I would totally agree with that! With that in mind, let's talk about avoiding the turnoffs.

While we are all trying build our brand or sell what we do (our products) to someone in some capacity or another, there are proper ways to go about selling yourself and trying to place your songs. Otherwise, if you're not careful, you can turn someone off and close a door ... permanently.

Should you happen to be fortunate enough to make some good initial connections or contacts, value and respect the connection more than your songs and more than your brand.

If you get an open door, and you are professional and courteous and respect people's time and leave them with a pleasant encounter, the chances are you will get an opportunity to be heard at a later date. Even better, you can possibly build a long-term relationship.

Timing Is Everything

Pitching songs isn't like selling your car. You're not going to talk someone into buying your car because you happen to be selling one. They have to actually be in need of a car. So talking about your car to someone who isn't in the market to buy one right now, well, it's a good way to have someone avoid you in the future.

You're not going to talk your new friend into placing your song, if now is not the right time. You're not going to convince them they're missing the greatest hit they've ever been pitched. In fact, attempting to convince them they need to hear your music and hear it NOW will cause you to lose favor with a professional contact.

That's one of the biggest turn offs for the non-songwriter that I've seen over the years. Certain songwriters want everyone to listen to three or four of their greatest songs, from beginning to end.

If you are making a new contact for placing a song, always ask if it is okay if you send them some of your material. Just because you made a new friend in the music business you don't have to send them your songs within the first week of meeting them. Especially if they have NEVER expressed the notion that they are looking for songs. Value and protect the potential for a relationship more than a possible song placement.

When to Follow Up on Your Pitches

If you do get a chance to share your songs, do not follow up dozens of times asking if they've listened to them.

Some writers do follow up a few weeks or months later to make sure the pitch was received. My philosophy has always been, if they're interested in what they hear, they'll let me know--and they always have!

I've never heard from 95% of the pitches for song placements I've made, but that is the nature of the game. (It's a numbers game, read the next chapter!) Some artists and labels receive hundreds and thousands of song demos. They can't respond to each and every one. They won't.

Okay, there was one time I did get a voice message from an iconic group who are Country Music Hall of Fame inductees. They were letting me know that they appreciated me sending songs for consideration on their new album, but they were going to "pass" on them.

It kind of faked me out, I thought they were calling to place a song on hold! It was still a very nice, courteous gesture, but one you will rarely have from anyone.

In fact, of all the years I've pitched songs, that was my only phone call for a pass on a song. I'm actually not acquainted with the artist. I've never been personally introduced to them, but I've been working around Nashville for many years, building my brand. When you put time and effort into networking and branding yourself, people will become aware of your brand.

Patience Is a Virtue

As a manager of an independent record label, I've been pitched thousands of songs from songwriters. I've had my share of songwriters who want to not only pitch me the songs, but tell me how and why they wrote them. In all actuality, your song should indicate all of that. If you have to tell that beforehand so people will "get" the song, a rewrite may be in order.

Aspiring songwriters tend to want to share how great they think their songs are. They tell me over and over that they KNOW the song would be a hit for this artist or that artist if they would just record the song. They go on and on about their songs. Even when I've said, "we're not looking for songs at this moment".

That is definitely a turnoff to the non-songwriters in the music industry.

I've had songwriters who would follow up on a regular basis. Weekly or monthly calls asking if I've listened to the songs or if I've shared them with any artists I'm working with. Or if I have listened, what I thought about them.

Some of the follow up was so excessive that it created a mental experience of dread for me whenever I saw their email or number pop up on my phone.

Again, excessive follow up or asking for advice or affirmation about the greatness of a song is a turn-off. And remember, the wheels of the music business move very, very slow. Just be patient.

Let the relationships build over time, don't rush them. Avoid the turn offs! Build your relationships, build your brand, and let the process unfold. You can't rush the process, but you CAN get yourself excluded from the process.

Here are some DO's and DON'Ts:

- Always be polite and conscious of the other person's time.

- State your purpose or reason for contact (if you're contacting someone), you can mention a few of your credits but keep it brief.

- If you're wanting to pitch songs, ask up front what type of songs they are possibly looking for, and if you may have their permission to share a few songs with them. Again, keep it brief. Don't send barn burning, up-tempo songs when someone is looking for a ballad, just because you have a great up-tempo number.

- Do not send more than two songs!

- Always include lyrics.

- If you feel the need to follow up, allow your new contact at least 2 weeks or longer, then follow up once and only once.

- Unless you're invited to do so, wait 3-6 months before you ask to submit other songs.

- Do not go on and on about how great the song or songs are. Let the listener make that assessment.

- If they do "pass" on your songs, do not ask for a critique or review of your songs or ask why. Be professional. You were one of hundreds or thousands, and some of those were professional songwriters who also had their material passed over. Be gracious and thank them for the opportunity.

The songwriting and music publishing business, if you want to put it in terms of "rejection", is about 99% rejection. So move on, keep plugging away, maintain and develop a good professional etiquette when working with others. It's a numbers game … read the next chapter.

Someone may not like your songs at the moment, but don't give them a reason to not like you as well!

CHAPTER 13: IT'S A NUMBERS GAME

Several years ago I was invited as a songwriter and music publisher to attend GMA's Immerse Conference (Gospel Music Association) in Nashville. I attended as an industry representative who would be available to aspiring songwriters to answer questions one on one. That event was really the catalyst for this book.

I participated in a luncheon attended by a few hundred people from all over the U.S and Canada. Several other industry representatives were in attendance and we each would spend 5-10 minutes at each table, answering as many questions as we could from the aspiring songwriters. Then we'd rotate to the next table.

One consistent question that came up was, "I wrote this song and I want to know how to do something with it." My first thought was, "A song? One song?"

It reminded me that over the years, it was one flaw I've always noticed first. They wrote one song and it was their "baby". They were probably never going to have any more "children" until that one became successful.

For some reason, there are aspiring writers who cannot move on from that one song. They want to pin an entire songwriting career on one song.

They tend to think that a famous artist should record their one song. They spend their time and energy trying to get one particular well-known artist who they are certain would have a "hit" if they recorded the song.

I will say flat out: it doesn't work that way. Songwriting is a numbers game. It's like a lottery ticket: you can't buy just one lottery ticket and expect to win the jackpot. It is mathematically possible, but it is very highly improbable. Having more lottery tickets helps increase your chances of winning.

A very wise music publisher friend gave me some good advice over 20 years ago: the songwriting business is a numbers game.

He had a songwriter who was getting a ton of songs recorded during the year. He also began to have other songwriters signed to his publishing company who were complaining about the disparity in the amount of cuts this songwriter was getting in comparison to their own.

My publisher friend actually did the math. He took the number of songs each writer was writing during a year and factored in the number of those songs that were getting recorded. Do you know what he found?

In regard to percentages, this songwriter wasn't getting any more cuts than anybody else! The difference was that he was writing over 50 songs a year ... about one a week. The other songwriters were turning in around 10 songs a year ... about one a month.

That means one writer was getting five to ten songs placed in a year while the others were getting one or two. Same placement percentages, just a difference in the volume of product being created.

Now before you started writing down any ole lyric and cranking out a song per day, these guys were all very good writers and were trying to write the best songs they could every time they wrote. It's just that one songwriter made himself available to writing and creating good songs much more often than the others.

The bottom line is you can't do much with your songs if you don't have very many songs to do anything with.

Songs literally become your inventory, and any good business has to have a good volume inventory on hand.

Imagine going into a huge grocery store and all they had, aisle after aisle was one product. Apples. Every aisle you went down simply had this one product, apples.

No other fruits, no vegetables, no boxes of cereal, no bread, no meat, no dairy, etc. They might sell a few apples, but I imagine most people would walk in and then walk right back out because they weren't looking for apples that day. Or maybe they just didn't like apples.

The point is, you need a catalog of songs that are a variety of tempos and a variety of styles. Songs that address a variety of subjects and tastes. The bigger your catalog of these types and varieties of good, well-written songs, the better mathematical chances you have of placing them or putting them to use.

The placement outlets today are far and wide. It's still possible to place songs with artists who are connected with certain genres of music. But it's also possible to have outlets for songs beyond radio hits and album cuts. In fact it's more probable.

Don't stop at writing a few songs, or simply targeting songs toward artists you like. Create products that sound like they could work in a documentary. Try writing songs about certain themes or topics--or practice writing a song for some type of imagined campaign.

For example, Chevy licensed and used the Bob Seger song, "Like A Rock", in its commercials to brand its trucks. Bob didn't write this for Chevy, it was on an album in 1986. The song title and theme were universal, it could apply to a person or an object like a Chevy truck.

Keep your **hook book** handy at all times. That's the writing tablet many songwriters carry around to jot down anything that sparks the idea for a song.

I actually use the Notes app in my iPhone. My phone is always with me. This way I keep multiple song ideas going at one time. Some of them I work on a few lines at a time when they inspire me, just for the constant mental exercise of working on lyrics. Others I save for co-writing sessions.

The bigger and more developed your repertoire of songs are, the greater your chances of placements become.

It's a numbers game, so you need the numbers!

Chapter 14: Do I Need a Publisher?

The answer to the question, "Do I need a music publisher?" is yes and no.

Most aspiring songwriters who are trying to place songs do not necessarily need a music publisher. Of course, a music publisher who is plugged in, has great connections and a good track record of getting songs placed is very valuable. However, most songwriters won't have the opportunity to land a writing deal or position with a music publisher of this status. Larger music publishers are looking for writers who have already built a track record.

Starting Your Own Music Publishing Company

The truth is: from where you sit as a songwriter who is building your brand and your catalog of songs, you can actually form and start your own music publishing company.

This requires that you submit the proper paperwork to your respective PRO (Performance Rights Organization) and clear a music publisher name of your choosing, as well as pay a registration fee.

ASCAP costs around $25 and BMI has a fee of $150 to register and start your own publishing company (fees may change over time). The PRO you select, must also match the PRO you are a member of as a songwriter.

Advantages of Having Your Own Music Publishing Company

I've had several music publishing companies over the years just to represent and house the songs I write. At times, if I've struck a deal on getting a song recorded, and it involved signing over a percentage of the publishing, I was able to transfer the publishing with an assignment of copyright.

Most often and even advantageous, I've been able to pitch songs to potential placement outlets as a music publisher and not just as a songwriter.

The Music Industry's Shift

I'm not discouraging anyone from looking for a deal with a music publisher. It is just the truth of the matter that songwriter deals are almost non-existent compared to a few decades ago.

During the 80's and 90's in Nashville, there were literally thousands of songwriters who had writing deals with music publishers. The music publisher would sign songwriters exclusively to either a contract based on a period of time or a certain number of songs and pay them a weekly or monthly draw, which was an advance against their future writers' royalties.

My point is, due to the changing nature of the music business, this "writing deal" for songwriters with music publishers has gone from a few thousand to just a few hundred ... and shrinking.

I know songwriters in fields like Gospel Music who sign exclusive songwriting deals with certain publishers, without receiving a draw or pay. They choose this route because certain publishers have developed a large circle of relationships and influence and are the go-to catalogs in their genre when artists or labels are looking for songs. Publishers in other genres are adopting similar practices. The songwriter gets paid when the song gets placed and royalties collected.

Things to Consider about Music Publishers

Should you ever have the opportunity to work with a music publisher, the main consideration is that you want the songs they publish to be well represented.

As a songwriter, the worst case scenario with a publisher is to have songs sitting in their publishing catalog that aren't being pitched for placement. They're simply one of hundreds or thousands of songs that are not being worked by the publisher.

I have a few of these myself, songs that are tied up in huge catalogs that aren't being actively pitched anymore. I've attempted to regain my copyrights, but the language of the contract doesn't allow for their return to the songwriter. Most publishers won't return the copyright to a songwriter; after all, they have time and money invested in them.

What to Expect if You Do Become Your Own Publisher

Being your own publisher isn't easy--it is in essence another hat you will wear, but it does have its advantages. I know songwriters typically fall on the creative side and running your own publishing catalog will require you to tap into the admin side of your brain.

You will need to educate yourself on some of the basics of music publishing. Creating single song contracts between yourself and your music publishing company. Registering those songs with your PRO through your online account. Keeping organized files on your catalog of songs with song contracts, lyric sheets, US copyright information (if you copyright your works), addresses and contact info for co-writers, etc.

Should you secure song placements, you will also be responsible for issuing a mechanical license, sync license, or permission for use of the song, whichever is applicable.

You will also be responsible for collecting any royalties and keeping accurate books as to what revenues you earn.

The upside to having your own publishing company is something I mentioned earlier, you can put on your music publisher hat and pitch songs as a publisher rather than a songwriter.

In the music business hierarchy, reaching out as a music publisher is a bit more well-received than simply reaching out as a songwriter. You definitely want to represent yourself as a music publishing company. The appearance as a "business" is important! You will want email addresses, websites, social media pages, letterhead, etc. that represent your music publishing company.

I can look back upon myself as a young songwriter 30 years ago and see how early involvement and education in forming and working with my own publishing catalogs allowed me to step back as a songwriter and distance myself a bit and see a bigger picture.

Imagine if you were an inventor, you've got some great ideas for new inventions or products, but then you also learn what it actually takes to bring those inventions to market.

You learn that you will need a factory to manufacture and produce the product. You'll need to know about how to sell and market the product, how to deliver the product and collect receivables.

Also imagine the difference in reaching out to someone and saying: "I'm an inventor and have some ideas for new products" or reaching out and saying: "I manufacture and distribute new products and want to share some of my catalog with you".

Over the past three decades I've done both. I've operated my own music publishing companies. They not only contain many of my own songs, but I've signed songs by other songwriters and hold many of my father's copyrights that I've placed over the years.

I've also written for and worked with several music publishers as a songwriter. My decisions were always made on a song-by-song basis as to which route would give a particular song its best chance for placement.

The answer to: "do I need a music publisher" is basically yes. But it doesn't mean you have to find an outside entity to have your songs represented. You can be your own music publisher. You can represent yourself as a music publisher.

Chapter 15: Find the Theme to Your Song

Now, it's time to come up with the actual lyrics to your song and for that, you will have to find a theme. At this stage, it is now easy to do so, since you've gathered enough keywords, all sounding and rhyming like you want them to.

First, you will have to look at your keywords and ask yourself what they all have in common. For instance, if your keywords are "give", "pleased", "gone" or "strong" your theme could easily end up being about "a rebellious lover". If you come up with words like "childhood", "memory", "play" or "sweet kisses", your theme will most likely be about "childhood memories", etc. So, it doesn't matter if you've come up with words that rhyme or just ordinary words, because, after all, this is how creativity works, it's unexpectable and in a good way. So, here what matters the most is how you connect your words (or keywords) in order to find your final theme.

Once you've found your theme, you will then have to start writing your lyrics (you will also see that this step is easier than it seems). But first, you have to remember a few things:

-One, a song is made up of a number of verses and a chorus (which is repeated several times during the song), so your text shouldn't be more than 500 words, especially when you want to work fast and get great results.

-Number two on our list, you will have to work following a certain methodology here. This means that you will write a story, by following the model below for the verses and the chorus of your song:

- **A determination part,** which will explain your state of mind or mood. This section reveals the theme of the song (other than the title of your song). This is where you reveal how you feel in a few words.

- **A plot or confirmation of intention**, where you will confirm what you know (you are the story teller so your imagination should be at work here). This portion concerns the chorus of your song.

- **One more verse** where you will talk more about the mood or your determination. Here, you will add more lines in continuation to your first verse, where you will tell more about your feelings and what you are going through.

- Number three, you will have to decide on how many verses you would like your song to have. The average number is two, but sometimes people will add a third verse, which is normally similar to the first one, but with a few modified (adding to the story and melody).

- Lastly, apart from the verses and the chorus, you will also have to decide if your song will have an instrumental portion also known, most of the time, as the solo guitar (but it may also consist of another instrument or other instruments). Or, if you will add a bridge to your song (this is optional), as a bridge often introduces a verse which announces hope, regrets, fun, etc., but with a different tone or melody as the other verses. The bridge normally consists of a few lines and is followed by the chorus nearing the end of the song.

Let's now take a few examples to see how each step unveils during that stage of your writing:

-Step one, the keywords (found in the previous stages) used to build the theme of the song: "Rage", "fear", "passion", "defeat ". Here, the theme could end up being **"A lover's indifference".**

-Step two, start writing a text (this is not your final lyrics because you may have to adjust them during later stages of your writing). The whole text should be under 500 words, and made up of a few simple sentences able to explain your theme, and follow this model (remember that for this example we've picked 'a lover's indifference" as a theme):

1.EXPLANATION

"I woke up this morning, alone again"

"This has become a habit; how can I complain"

"Feeling pain, but I can't leave you, who is to be blamed"

"Baby, how can I please you, and reignite the flame"

*Note how easy it is to come up with words after defining the theme and following a song structure (explanation, confirmation/plot, further explanation). And with some small sentences you are able to find rhymes (if you wish to) and stay true to the theme, which is clearly explained, but in a creative way. Your verses can be as long as you wish them to be, but remember that 500 words are ideal if you want to write a well-structured song in only a day. So, write an intro which will constitute an explanation of the theme like the 5 lines above, and then decide how you are going to introduce the chorus. Here, you have two options:

a-A keyword that will sound different than the other lines and which will have a direct link to the chorus.

b-A small paragraph (which is also part of the first verse), of maybe two lines, which will serve as a conclusion to the first few lines of the verse and an introduction to the chorus. This is called a Pre-chorus, as it serves as a transition between a verse and a chorus.

2-THE CHORUS: This part should confirm a plot, an intention or a situation. Remember that you are supposed to tell a story and at the same time make sure it goes well with the music that will form part of the song when you hit the studio. But, you still have to let your ideas flow here (by flowing we mean let your imagination be at work). Remember to write small sentences under the theme ""**A lover's indifference"**. So, as an example, the chorus will be:

"Gave you love, but now you've changed"

"I've stayed by your side, but got nothing but pain".

"My heart is aching, I can't believe this is how things are"

"Let me know what is going on because my heart is aching"

*The chorus here is very explanatory and short, but it's easy to sing along too. When you write your chorus, you have to think about how many voices will be involved with singing it and how you can harmonize it with your wording. Again, you could have made it a bit shorter or slightly longer, all that matters is that you remember that the text should not be more than 500 words.

3-THE SECOND VERSE: This comes after the chorus is supposed to complete the first verse, by still following the same theme and the same structure as the first verse (by perhaps keeping the rhymes if you want to or go for a free writing style). It is supposed to explain the author's or singer's theme a bit more like the following (remember to keep the text engaging and help listeners plunge into your universe and maybe help them understand the song a little bit more):

"What is this that you want, baby"

"Didn't I give you all that you need"

"Could it be that you've changed your mind baby"

"Set me free, like the air that I breathe"

*Note that here again, we've come up with easy sentences, that rhyme (like with the first verse and that a continuation of the first verse, with the same intensity). Here, we are still following the same structure explanation/plot or situation/further explanation, for an easy flow of words.

4-THE BRIDGE (optional): Remember the bridge is that small section where you either want to introduce a passage of hope, regret or grief (with respect to the structure explanation/plot or situation/ further explanation). If you choose to write a bridge for your song, it would have to describe hope, grief, etc., or again, something that constitutes an open door or a big question mark. These are just suggestions, so that your writing becomes faster and that you don't give up your work. So, here's a suggestion for our bridge:

"Maybe I was wrong from the very beginning"

"Hope someday you'll open up and find someone you'll love"

"Unconditionally, it could have been me"

"This is how it's going to be"

"I just can't keep on like this, I need real love"

*After this part, you are supposed to carry on with the chorus or add a third verse that will maybe resemble the first one, but with a few different words like:

"I woke up this morning, <u>and it was cold</u> again"

"This has become a habit; how can I complain"

"Feeling pain, but I know <u>I miss you</u>, who is to be blamed"

"Baby, how can I please you, and reignite <u>your</u> flame"

Let's try this technique with one more example:

1-Kewords and Theme: Peace, rich, sharing. Here the theme could be **"Justice in the world"**

2-First Verse explanation: Short sentences making sure that you don't go above 500 words.

"Children dying"

"Young men Crying"

"I've lost some sleep last night"

"Why are we so selfish"

"Isn't it obvious"

"that the world has come to an end"

3-A chorus: Bring in the plot/ a situation, etc.,

"No more war!"

"I say no more war!"

"Where is the justice?"

"Today, I want no more war!"

4-A second verse: More explaining, again a short text with short sentences.

"I use to think that men were good"

"But, then why is there so much pain?"

"World politics, it worse than it used to"

"Democracy is no difference than Anarchy"

"People wake up and say"

5-A chorus, followed by a bridge (optional):

"Let's come together"

"Today, everywhere, anyone"

"Let's come together"

"Black or white, rich and poor"

6-One last verse (also optional):

"Keep your money"

"But, don't you forget, the blood of the innocent souls"

"I don't want to vote if my vote equals pain"

"I'd rather be with my brothers of peace"

7-Followed by the chorus.

So, by the end of this phase, you will be able to come up with a text which will constitute 80% of your final work, because even if you have to make rectification during later stages of your writing, not much of the text will be changed. This portion of your writing is perhaps the longest and can last up to 5 hours. Make sure you get some beverages that will help you focus, or take short breaks of 10 minutes, where you will close your eyes and try to re-energize yourself.

- All you have to retain from this chapter is that:

- Your song should have different parts namely a first verse, a chorus, a second verse, a bridge (optional), and a third verse (also optional).

- You must use the keywords, you've found during previous stages to build a solid theme.

- The theme must then serve to help you write a story that will follow this structure: Explanation or mood/ confirmation of mood or situation/ and further explanation of the story

- Sometimes you may want to add up a bridge, which should tell more about the author's grief, hopes, etc., but this portion is optional.

- Lastly, always remember that you have a limited amount of words that you should work with, in just one day. This number is 500 and you should try not to go beyond that number.

Chapter 16: Adjust the Wording to the Rhythm

This next chapter is about adjusting your text to the rhythm you've already worked on. You remember how you've recorded your sang syllables earlier right? Here, you will use that recording, by using the tapping technique and singing your song mentally. This means that the only melody that should be heard here is the one you've recorded earlier. Let's begin:

-First, play your sang syllables once.

-Replay this portion of your song and start tapping 1, 2, 3, 4 on your lap, or with your foot.

-Now, combine the record (play it a third time), with your wording, and the tapping. Mimic the syllables and try to match your wording with your initial arrangement.

If you feel that one of your sentences is too short, add a word or two, and replay that line. This means that each of your lines should match your 1, 2, 3, 4 tap at the end of your syllables and if a line stops at 2, or 3, you will have to add a word, so it can match your last syllable (or reach 4). The same goes when a line is too long and it goes beyond 4 (meaning that you will end up counting 1,2,3,4,5 and maybe more). Here again, you will have to rework your wording. The key to making it an effective task is by keeping the same meaning all by following the rhythm and, above all, respect the theme. Now, note that each number corresponds to a singing note, a group of words, a group of word corresponding to a singing technique, etc., so think about it when you start singing.

Let's see an example to illustrate all that:

With the theme "A lover's indifference".

First verse: "I woke/ up this morning/, alone/ again"

Rhythm count: 1 /   2   / 3   / 4
Good

Or it can also go like this (depending on your rhythm):

"I woke/ up/ this morning/, a/lone/ a/gain"

Rhythm count: 1   / 2/ 3   /4 / 5   /6 / 7.

Then, there might be too many words in your verse. So, correct it.

Instead of "I woke/up/this morning/, a/lone/ a/gain", you might rethink of ways on how to sing this verse once again and make sure your line can be counted in four, when you tap your feet on the floor like this: "I woke/ up this morning/, alone/ again". Or perhaps rewrite it so that it can now fit your initial rhythm, like for instance "Got up today by myself again", this sentence has less words than the original sentence, and "got up" and "by myself" make up a wording of two words that sound better when sang together, so it should be: "Got up/ today/ by myself/ again",

Rhythm count: 1 / 2 / 3 / 4 ,

Here, you should do this for the verses or chorus that made up your initial melody and arrangement (remember that the piece of melody you've worked on earlier only consists of a small portion that were stuck in your mind). Now it's time to fit the rest of the song to the rest of the melody and work on it as shown above.

Make sure you use the same technique, line after line, for each verse, the chorus and the bridge (if you decide to add one). This part can take a few minutes if you are very focused and engaged with your writing and the song, but overall, take your time until you are satisfied with the results.

After this stage, you are almost done with your song, as you will have reworked the wording and fit it with your initial arrangement.

- What you should remember about chapter 5 is that:

- One, go through your arrangement. Go through the whole thing in order to get in the mood again.

- Two, introduce your rhythm (the 1,2,3,4 tap) and sing mentally (no voice on your behalf at this point, as the singing, should be in your head).

- Three, adjust the wording with the Rhythm count (1,2,3,4) and if wording overlaps (goes beyond 4) or if it's too short (stops at 2 or 3), adjust your wording, but make sure that you keep the same meaning in the song.

- The rhythm counting is a metered writing technique where the wording you pick corresponds to your rhythm arrangements, meaning that when you count to 4, you should be singing your last note or last group of words (corresponding to the same key or singing technique).

With that said, let's now move on to our last phase of the writing.

CHAPTER 17: CREATIVITY

CREATIVITY WITH FORM

As a songwriter, it's fine to think of yourself as a creative artist, but it's also useful to think of yourself as a craftsman (or craftswoman!). With this mindset, like a furniture maker, or carpenter -- songwriters have the chance to explore all of their materials, (formal) designs, and techniques as they make up new tunes. Thinking about your song in this way will also help you learn these techniques more quickly from other songwriters.

Creative people tend to seek inspiration from all around themselves!

Let's try a mind experiment with song form.

So if you think of the process of songwriting as similar to building a solid table, a comfortable dining room chair, or even a great backyard tool shed for your lawnmower and rakes -- there are some interesting parallels to writing music.

So read through this list, but think about the current song that you're working on right now:

Designing a table

- ☐ How many legs does it need to be able to stand?
- ☐ Will it have a central base instead of individual legs?
- ☐ Will it be square, round, rectangular, or oval shaped?

- Will it have extenders that can be added to the middle of your table to make it larger for more guests, and if so, how does it maintain its original strength in the new position?
- What's the function of the table - is it for work, the dining room, or just to hold a lamp next to the couch?

Designing a chair

- How many legs does it need?
- Will it be a stationary design, rocking chair, or a swivel design?
- Will the chair be adjustable or just designed with a fixed height?
- How high will the back of the chair go and will the back be connected to the legs?
- Will the chair have arms or be open?
- How can you make it strong enough to support most anyone?

Designing a tool shed

- How big will the overall shed be?
- What about the design of the base (cement slab?) and the roof?
- Will it just be for storage, or will it also have a small work table or work bench inside?
- How will you enter the shed?
- Will it have a single door, double door, and more than one entrance?
- And does the back door need a ramp for the lawnmower?

- Where will the tools go -- will there be pegboards, shelves, or other storage?
- Will it have windows?

Okay, so what does all of this carpentry have to do with songwriting?

I think craftsmen think about this stuff in advance, and songwriters often just plow ahead! Sure that can work, but sometimes you look at your basic idea, see where it's at, decide where you want it to be, and then do some real planning!

If you're like me, just thinking about those obvious questions related to furniture or carpentry regarding design in my songwriting leads me to all sorts of interesting ideas!

Form And Design

So let's talk more about form.

Form is that aspect of songwriting that doesn't get enough attention. Our shed, table, or chair examples above would likely fall without some real planning concerning structure, layout, and formal design.

Of course, many examples of high art -- music, books, poetry, films, paintings, plays, and sculpture -- all have a solid sense of form. Even if you can't see the structure -- it's virtually invisible -- it's what helps the piece hold together.

So with that said, here are some interesting exercises in creativity that should inspire you:

Take two or three of your all-time favorite cover songs and using a blank sheet of paper, map out their entire forms. Try it: Find the INTRO, VERSE, BRIDGE, CHORUS, VERSE, BRIDGE, CHORUS, BRIDGE 2, CHORUS, SOLO, CHORUS, for example. Once you've done this with a few tunes, you'll soon discover the "modular' nature of your favorite songs -- these beautiful tunes. You might even realize that you're not creating enough distinct components in your songs.

ASK YOURSELF:

- How long are the intros?
- What's the length of the verses compared to the chorus?
- Are the verses always the same length?
- Does the piece ever change key (modulate), and if so at what STRUCTURAL point?
- Are there any structural surprises?
- Are the "modules" consistent regarding mood, tone, or even energy?
- What else can we notice about the structure?

Now let's talk about your lyrics.

Creativity With Lyrics

How often do you study lyrics by your favorite songwriters and lyricists? There is so much to learn there, and even if you prefer to let someone else write lyrics for your songs, it's useful to truly understand the craft.

So here are some ideas to help you, concepts to inspire you, and tips to assist you as you write lyrics for your songs:

- I think everyone who is writing lyrics has to have a dedicated notebook and keep it with them at all times -- or at least very close by! Anytime you hear an unusual phrase in conversation, have a quick story idea for lyrics, or just listen to a single word that suggests an image or concept to you -- you need to capture it by writing it down.
- Many musicians write songs until they get stuck, and then stop for the day. No! If you're writing lyrics, and you get stuck on a particular word -- especially if you're just searching for a workable rhyme, plug in any word so that you can keep moving! Don't allow any rough patch and hard decision to stop you from writing the rest of the song or to break your momentum. (Some fiction authors do this by putting the phrase the letters "TK" in their manuscript ("to come"), so they can just keep going!
- Study lyrics by all of your favorite artists and songwriters and read them aloud, both with and without the melody.
- In the lyrics by your favorite songwriters, consider the possibilities (good and bad) if you change a single word? It's an incredible

lesson! Even look at a list of the greatest songs ever written -- there are several very subjective lists available all over the web -- and consider changing a single word in each title. Once you do, let your creativity run with all of the changes in meaning that arise from that substitution. Try this when you're stuck!

- Study poetry from some different sources, both contemporary and historical, and notice the turns of phrase, the language choices, the imagery, the meter, the pacing, and more. Just observe.- Now take a piece of historical poetry that speaks to you and change the words to modern language but preserve the same meaning. If it's about love lost, that's easy and universal -- if it's about a location, make it about where you live. This is a tricky "exercise" but can inspire many new songs...

- Another lyric activity -- take one of your favorite songs and sing along with all of the verses and choruses, and then before the song is over -- stop the music and write original lyrics to a new verse in the same style, mood, and tone. Creating this additional verse is pretty challenging, but very rewarding. After you've written one good verse, go back to the original song's chorus or bridge/chorus, and go back and write another original verse.

- Another fun lyric exercise is to take any famous movie title, and ignore what the original film was about and just write some new lyrics based on what is suggested by the phrase alone. Imagine an entirely different story, brand new characters, and a new direction for the entire idea. This one gets my creativity flowing... (Seriously, tell me that last movie you watched? Cool title for your new song! Now write it!!)
- Imagine a character from a book or film that's not a musical and write a song from their perspective! This process is fun as well and works all over the place to bring you to new, fresh song ideas.

Now let's talk about creativity in your music.

CREATIVITY WITH MUSIC

The music chords, harmonies, and melodies of songs are my favorite parts of writing! (Probably because I'm a guitarist first...) I like to come up with new interesting chord progressions or catchy melody lines, and then just see where that leads me with lyrics and title.

Here are some music related exercises that will help songwriters get more out of their creativity:

- Take an existing song that you love (or hate!), and write all new chords and melodies while keeping the original lyrics. Treat them as a brand new set of words sent to you by a collaborator and start from absolute scratch. (This is fun and challenging, because it's hard to leave the identity, sound, and chords of the original tune.) You can even do this with one of your tunes... Set it an entirely new way. This is a great test for your songwriting chops!

- Whenever you can't seem to work on your music, I encourage you to try a whole range of songwriter exercises to enhance your imagination. So try writing music for one of your favorite poems (or find a famous one!) -- not to publish, but just for the challenge! It can even just be more modern poetry that's closer to your writing style, but either way, it can be very fun and challenging.

- I encourage every songwriter to explore some basic music theory and harmony, but in case you don't see the need -- check this out. Every key has a big cadence chord built on V and going to I major, or I minor. If you regularly write songs in a set key and want to stretch out chromatically (chromaticism is colorful!), then try cadence chords (V-I) to every other chord in the same key. For example, in C major the other chords are Dm, Em, F, G, Am, and Bdim. The same way G or G7 will cadence or resolve to C (V to I), there is a possibility of V's of all these other chords (A or A7 to Dm; B to Em; C to F, D to G, E to Am, and F# to Bdim). You can do these without changing keys, and they help add some impressive passing chords and chromatics. (In case you want to explore more, they're technically called "Secondary Dominants" and they can also involve bII or seven-diminished cadences, but that's for another book!)

- I like to take songs I've written or songs by others and convert a lot of the chords to SLASH chords. (No, not the guitar dude from Guns & Roses!) I mean wherever I have a D going to an A, those chords are in root position, I experiment with the sound of D/A going to an A triad. D/A means a D triad over an "A" root, which is a "slash" chord because it's written with a slash (/) and it's just an inversion -- meaning a D triad (D-F#-A) with its fifth in the bass. Where this gets interesting is when you use slash chords all over the place. So try your D major to A major like this: D/F# to A/C#, or D/E to A/B, or D to A/D... the possibilities are endless! It's a different sound but very common in gospel, blues, jazz, and r&b, but it fits everywhere!

- Jazz musicians regularly do this exercise, but it's ideal for all songwriters in any style. Keep the original song and all of its melody notes, but change all the chords. This process is called reharmonization, and it makes the music sound very different, very fresh, and entirely new. Here's how it works: if you have a C major chord with a "G" in the melody, that's obviously the fifth of the chord, but you might try that spot in the tune with an A minor chord (making the "G" the seventh of the new chord), or an F Maj (making the melody the ninth of the new chord). This is a great way to expand your ears into new harmonies. The melody is the same, but the effect is different. (Many pop/rock artists do this for unplugged versions, orchestral settings, or just old tunes that need to be updated!)

- The next idea is to bend your chords -- not with a whammy bar, or keyboard pitch wheel, but by changing any note by a half-step up or down. This can make your melodies do kind of interesting things and may send your song off in an entirely new direction. So with an A major triad (A-C#-E), see if it fits your music to bend the E up to an F (to an A+), or the C# down to a C (making an A2 chord). Lot's of possibilities here, if not just for chords and melodies, but for movement during intros, interludes, and codas.

- Try this -- take any and all of the music ideas that you start with and change it to a parallel minor. So if you have a section in B major, try the same thing again in B minor, keeping the intervals relatively similar. This is a good way to help develop your ideas and take your song to a new sound world.

- This one is about your melody. When you listen to a song by one of the masters, have you ever considered where the highest note of the song occurs? Does the artist ever go higher? Sometimes a song will start "low and slow" for the intro and first verse, and just get higher until that big soaring note in the chorus. Often it's possible that there's an even higher note in the bridge to reach even deeper emotionally. So in your music, think about your melodic range, and perhaps plan it out a bit. Maybe even delay getting to that big important note and see where that leads. It might be just what your song needs.

- Speaking of the bridge section of your tunes, consider how it can be such a completely new musical place in the 'architecture' of your song. (Listen for the many examples of this in the great songwriters of the past!) One way is just to introduce all new harmonies and go to a very distant sound world once you get there -- with the challenge being the return to the chorus afterward. If all new chords feel too remote for your piece, try choosing a simple harmony from the beginning parts of your song (intro, verse, chorus) and make that the new tonic, tonal center, or center of gravity. Then, at least, the chord sounds familiar, you're just suddenly making it more important and central.

Chapter 18: Become a Professional Songwriter

If you want to become a songwriter -- and make this your primary occupation -- that's a fantastic goal and a big journey. I want to help point you in the right direction with several things to think about, and some useful resources to check out -- but some of this is beyond the focus of this short book. I encourage you to visit many of the websites listed on our resource page and read absolutely everything you can about the business of songwriting, and the music industry in general.

What Does It Take?

In the most simplistic terms, what creates a full-time income as a songwriter is a large enough body of work that actively generates royalties, and other residual income to meet all of your monthly expenses. If you have a growing catalog that is recorded, and regularly produces significant broadcast royalties (ASCAP, BMI, or SESAC), you will be able to sustain yourself as a songwriter through your quarterly payments. Of course, to create a song catalog that is both extensive enough, and active enough to create a full-time income, it takes a balance between active, current projects and a valuable back catalog.

Professional songwriters also supplement their writer royalties with publishing royalties. If you self-publish or co-publish your works, you'll have a better chance of building up sustainable living-wage royalties faster. The problem is that generally the projects that generate the most lucrative writer royalties -- for example, your song recorded by a major recording artist -- usually require some negotiation (or surrendering!) of any publishing royalties.

For those composer/lyricists who are also performers, musicians, and singers, then you also have the support from live gigs, performances, and mechanical royalties from performances on the recording. For those who want to write exclusively, songwriting teams, collaborators, and individual projects might be just the sort of professional activities that it takes to diversify your income.

Action Steps: The first step to becoming a full-time professional songwriter is to understand the industry, your rights, royalty structures, and to have sufficient professional contacts to have viable demand for your songs. Most professional songwriters take a long-term view of their careers and build a body of work or catalog to sustain them through lean years. Of course, we only hope, wish, pray or dream for that huge hit song that goes global -- gets tons of airplay, wins awards, and gets used in a blockbuster Hollywood film, but the reality is to try to create a full-time income and living wage first. If you can sufficiently generate $40K, $50K, or $75K every year as a songwriter, then you have more of a chance of creating that large valuable catalog of songs, compositions, and lyrics. So step one, although this is not a personal finance book, is to figure out what you would need to survive comfortably and work backward. If you had a goal of $50K in annual royalties as a songwriter (including any gigs, publishing rights, and special projects), then you would know that each quarterly payment from your performing rights society must be $12,500. Another way to look at this is $50K divided by 52 weeks in the year means that your songs (and music career overall) need to generate $961.54 each week or $4166 per month. Strange as it seems, seeing the exact number always motivates me!

In the pages that follow we'll discuss rights, royalties, and piracy (briefly), and then have a discussion about the useful habits of a professional songwriter. Then, there's a short resource page to help you find out lots more about this business of songwriting.

So let's get started.

RIGHTS, ROYALTIES, AND PIRACY

If you want to be successful as a songwriter, you need to know as much about the business of songwriting as possible - largely because that's how you get paid! That's what we'll touch on a little bit here, but please be sure to check out the resources page for more sites, organizations, and other ideas to get you started.

Rights, Royalties, and Piracy

The U.S. Copyright Office in Washington, DC is an excellent source of information for creative people, especially songwriters, because they spell out the current laws related to your intellectual property rights. If everything you know about copyright is based on myths, fables, and wives tales, then you may be living in FEAR over the theft of your new songwriting masterpiece. (If you reside outside the U.S., make sure that you have a solid understanding of the copyright laws in your country -- some are much stronger than ours!)

The truth is that copyright issues are constantly in FLUX, and there's a significant current problem with PIRACY and that many of these matters change on a regular basis -- that's why I would rather point you to some important websites rather than include material here that could quickly go out of date. Be sure to check out the copyright information first!

Piracy

So the "piracy" issue includes books and media (CDs, DVDs, etc.) that have been released both in an original, official version AND also in counterfeit or "pirated" versions that are meant to trick the consumer into thinking they're buying the original, authentic product. What's the problem, you ask? More sales, more word of mouth, and a bigger fan base, right? Isn't that a good thing?

Yes, and no. Sure films, books, and CDs might pick up a few more long-term fans based on a pirated copy, but the correct supply chain will not ever see those revenues or profits. The artist, label, musicians, distributors, and others won't accurately get credited for any sales that happen this way. And for musicians who had received an advance or signing bonus when they got their deal, they need real, legitimate sales to earn that money back for the recoup.

Where most songwriters and musicians worry too much is in the theft of their individual songs. "Oh no, someone might steal my latest treasure..."

But let's look at this another way. Here's the scariest part of theft, copyright, and piracy.

FEAR.

How about this: C.P.L.I.F.?

(Or the scary idea of "Creative People Living In Fear"...)

Some talented musicians and songwriters never fully develop their craft, or their careers because they're always too concerned with someone stealing their music. They can be so scared that they never share their music in useful ways that could open up doors of opportunity.

What you should understand is that if you write a great song as a songwriter and lyricist, and send it around to see if people would be interested in performing it or recording it, you need to let others hear it.

If it gets recorded, you will get paid -- there are royalties that cover this (called mechanical and broadcast royalties, but that's a big fat topic!). And if someone wants to use your song in a movie, TV commercial, or somewhere online -- they'll usually just license it -- paying you a fee for usage.

But realize this:

In this day and age, no major label recording artist needs to actually "steal" your song.

They won't do it.

It's bad for business, and for their career, and because of the money involved in royalties they'd much rather actually just record their original music. And labels have rights administrators that will take care of any paperwork if you do get your piece onto their next record.

And if they want to record your song, and you refuse to license it (for some reason!), they likely just find or compose a song that's relatively similar (but without infringement!), and you won't get anything.

Why do you think so many artists play their music openly on YouTube, Vimeo, or SoundCloud, and other sites? Because in general, theft of songs is rare, and they would rather play their songs and launch their careers rather than worrying about it.

Performing and Broadcast Rights

Songwriting is a lucrative business. There -- we said it! When you write a song that gets heavy airplay, you can make serious royalties, and that's why the music business is designed with this model in mind. (Sure selling records/CDs/mp3s and concert tickets matters a lot, but radio/TV money is massive!)

Royalties related to airplay and performance are tracked by the three big performing rights societies in the U.S. These are ASCAP, BMI, and SESAC, and their job is to credit performances, airplay, and broadcasts of registered music to composers, songwriters, and publishers. They follow the music in any venue and media that generates royalties --

mostly radio, TV, internet, and individual live performances, festivals, and tours. (Performing rights societies of several other countries are listed below.) Once collected, these royalties are paid out -- most often quarterly -- to the songwriters, authors/lyricists, and publishers.

In the United States, this includes receiving royalties from

the big three major TV networks: CBS, NBC, and ABC

The PBS television network (and other affiliates as well as the NPR radio stations

The Telefutura and Univision networks, and their related stations

Other local TV, cable programs, and cable systems

Local commercial radio, non-commercial radio, and satellite radio

Various websites (involved in streaming and broadcast)

Background music systems (for businesses, and airlines)

Colleges and universities

Concert presenters (some venues, festivals, and halls)

Symphony orchestras

Plus bars, hotels, restaurants, circuses, theme parks, and skating rinks

Across the globe, performing rights societies in other countries represent their composers, songwriters, and lyricists and usually have a "reciprocal" agreement with their American counterparts ASCAP, BMI, or SESAC to collect royalties for performances in the United States. For foreign songwriters, or American songwriters with performances and broadcasts across the globe, your earnings are collected by

SOCAN (Canada)

PRS for Music/MCPS (United Kingdom)

UBC (Brazil)

GEMA (Germany)

TONO (Norway)

JASRAC (Japan)

APRA-AMCOS (Australia) and many, many others around the world.

Once collected, the "reciprocal" arrangements mean that ASCAP, BMI, or SESAC will get these international royalties and distribute them to you -- usually quarterly.

ASCAP (The American Society of Composers, Authors, and Publishers), SESAC and Broadcast Music Inc (BMI) each have their strengths and benefits, so I won't make any specific recommendations here as to which one you should join. But you need to be in a performing rights society!

Each of the three performing rights societies has writers, lyricists, and publishers from all styles of music from rock to hip-hop, country to jazz, classical to pop. I will say that personally I've been a long-time member of ASCAP -- both as a writer and publisher -- and have a close friend who writes very similar things as I do, and has been in BMI for just as long. We're both happy with our choices. So bottom line -- you have to decide for yourself.

But how?

I always suggest that you look at the websites of all three societies (in the U.S.) and see what songwriters, composers, and lyricists are affiliated with each one, and use that as one way to help guide you. It's also possible to look at any sheet music, music books, or CD/album covers you have and get an idea where your favorite artist's songs are registered. Use those as a clue as well...

Once you join one of these three, then you must REGISTER all of your songs -- including each time you write a new one! It's not a complicated process, but you need to have your songs in their database -- and assigned a number -- so they can be tracked, and you can get paid.

Now let's take a look at habits that might help you to become professional with your songwriting...

PROFESSIONAL SONGWRITER HABITS

 Of course, professional songwriters' habits vary so widely that what you'll find here is a set of general suggestions to inspire your development. These tips will help you expand

and grow as a writer regarding creativity, productivity, and your overall effectiveness.

YOU SHOULD WRITE EVERY SINGLE DAY

It's pretty simple: Just write every day — every single day.

Why?

With practice, you'll get much, much better; it's that simple.

I knew a musician who wrote a little piano prelude each morning — just for himself — while the coffee was brewing. He did this ritual just to start his day with an exercise in creativity. He wasn't even a piano player, but as a composer, he chose that instrument for the range, the color, and the possibilities.

For him, this was just an exercise in natural self-expression, a chance to invent new melodies, and a way to explore harmonies and colors inside his ideas. He got into this habit of making short daily piano works based on his morning mood, energy, and thoughts.

After a while, he had a lot of these little pieces, and of course, many of them were just so-so. He wasn't trying to write masterpieces, but just to write. He wanted to simply create or compose on a regular basis without ever worrying about whether the pieces would be good enough to keep. It was coffee-brewing time, and it was a way to use his time more productively. But this is what he found. Out of the dozens and dozens of pieces he had to choose from, there were enough that were quite good that he was able to pull them into a set of pieces and have them all played together.

This creative routine is an excellent idea for songwriters, too. Make a daily ritual of your writing. It makes this process more common, more professional. You are getting up and going to work. It also protects you from being way too precious about your songs.

How?

Imagine that you spend your whole life trying to write one great song. You start, you stop. You finish a couple, but they're just okay. You judge your work too harshly and compare it to the best songs you've ever heard -- which is always a huge mistake. (Masterpieces by other songwriters are for inspiration — not for comparison!)

You're lost in a creative spiral because you're chasing a masterpiece. That singular perfect piece of music and poetry that delivers the complete message in an excellent intro-verse-chorus format to the listener is hard to write. You want it to have a great story, a wonderfully catchy melody, and an infectious hook. But it needs to be perfect. Well, it's almost impossible. Not because of some judgment of your skills, your talent, or your abilities -- no, because the being consumed with the thought of making the 'perfect song' is distracting to the efficient, creative process.

Aim high, of course, but thinking more like a craftsman is often a better overall attitude. Make a good, solid, wonderful song that feels right, holds together well, and gets the job done. Don't cut corners, and always make something you can be proud of, but just make well-crafted songs.

Then if you write a thousand songs, maybe you will have your masterpiece or two. You might find your hit songs, or whatever your ultimate goals are with your music. You can do this! Imagine that you start to write on a consistently regular basis and now finish one new song a month. Maybe you can even develop that up to a new song every two weeks, or even every week! (And professionals often have a more demanding production schedule than that.)

Don't you think your chances of writing a magnificent song are so much higher if you worked through and wrote a dozen (or 24, or 52) songs by the end of the year? Sure it takes much work and discipline -- but I prefer to say it just takes better habits. Just write something every day - lyrics, chords, bridge, titles, etc.

And I think it's easier, more fun, and more logical than trying to write and rewrite one piece over and over again and make it into your masterpiece.

Pro Songwriters Know Their Strengths

If you're a genius with lyrics, but can never seem to finish the music, or if you can make up great chord progressions and melodies, but can never get the words right, consider writing with a songwriting partner. You might find that the momentum of collaboration helps you finish a lot more material as well. Why? It's funny how often we'll let ourselves down with a deadline, but many people work hard not to disappoint someone else.

Many amazing songs have been written by more than one person, including the standard composer/lyricist pairing or by entire bands. If you're serious about what you're doing, you might also need an extremely dedicated writing partner, so be sure to spell that out in advance — that you're professional and productive. Often it takes longer to find the right collaborator, and you will have to be willing to write a few things together as a trial partnership with some of your 'candidates.'

And lastly, every musician — guitarists, pianists, singers, drummers, songwriters, and others — need to continue to learn about music. Spend some time exploring harmony, learn and study theory, read a broad range of books on music and creativity (thanks again for reading this!), and study anything that's useful to your art and craft!

Professional creatives learn from others as much as possible. That means that aside from other musicians, composers, lyricists, and songwriters, you should seek out inspiration from novelists, filmmakers, painters, poets — anyone whose creativity could inspire you in your pursuit.

Chapter 19: Do I Need To Copyright My Songs?

A work is under copyright protection the moment you create it. What copyright registration does is give your work a public record and a certificate of registration with US Copyright office.

The act of copyrighting your song is fairly easy. The steps to take are simple.

1. Make a copy of your song in some form, either by recording the lyric and melody on a CD, USB drive, MP3, a video, or write out the sheet music. All of these methods create a hard copy of your song.
2. Go to Copyright.gov and click on the Electronic Copyright Office link and make an online copyright filing.
3. You will need to create a "new user" account providing your name, address and country, phone number, and a preferred contact method.
4. Click on "Register a New Claim" under "Copyright Service" and answer questions about yourself, the work you're seeking to copyright and where you'd like the copyright certification to be sent.
5. Then you will need to pay the $35 fee either by credit card, debit card or electronic check.

6. Upload the electronic copy of your work. (You can also print out the forms and file by US Mail, which has a higher fee.)

With all that said, to answer the question of whether you NEED to copyright your song with the US Copyright Office or not is simply up to you.

In my personal songwriting career, I've never used the US Copyright Office to register my songs. Many songwriters I know do not register their songs, while others do. Typically major music publishers will apply for copyright registration, because they have the budget to do so.

You can see that at $35 per song, registering copyrights on songs can become quite expensive. I've only weighed out copyright registration and assessed the need for it on a song-by-song basis.

If I have a song that appears to be on the verge of major exposure in the commercial music world, then I consider copyright registration.

However, in this modern digital age, a digital footprint of a song can be made in numerous places that provide dates and proof of creation should the legal need arise to challenge a copyright infringement.

Personally, I post many of my demos to online entities such as SoundCloud.com, YouTube, my websites, Facebook videos and other outlets. I do this mainly for the ease of sending a link to pitch songs or give them public exposure. But this also shows dates and times of works I've created.

I also register my songs with my PRO. In my experience, I've had songs recorded by artists and was not made aware the songs were used. Registering with my PRO ensured that my song would be correctly accounted for in regard to performance royalty disbursements, should it receive any airplay.

If you have unlimited funds and want to copyright your songs, by all means copyright them. But if you're like most songwriters, it's not in the budget to pull the trigger on $35 per song.

I've met many aspiring songwriters who have an unfounded fear of having their songs stolen. It's not something I've ever worried about.

To be honest, of the hundreds of songwriters I've known over the years, I haven't met one who has had their song "stolen".

Even if a song is ripped off or stolen, it's a long, hard legal battle with a lot of legal costs involved to even prove there was copyright infringement. And it's a hard case to prove.

The biggest issue with songwriting, should you ever find yourself fortunate enough to have a song placed in a revenue producing position, is collecting royalties. Not someone stealing your song.

If copyrighting your songs is not in your budget, just make sure you have other proof of your work. Create single song contracts with dates and a witness (with the lyric attached), register your songs with your PRO (Performance Rights Organization), make demos of your songs and utilize outlets such as SoundCloud or other online outlets to show you are the creator of the songs.

Put aside any fears of "song theft". It rarely happens. If ever.

Song Outlets – Get Out Of The Box!

The Tried and True Methods
The traditional path of a songwriter has been to pitch their songs to artists, record labels and producers. Another pursuit has been to collaborate with writers who have a larger network of contacts in the hopes of getting a song placed through a co-write.

If you wish to incorporate these traditional methods in order to place songs, you can seek out various organizations or entities that may aid you in your quest.

For example, I've had a RowFax.com membership in the past. Each week or month they listed not only major Country labels or artists that were looking for songs, but many of the independent artists and labels as well.

In conjunction with that, I've had memberships with the Country Music Association (CMA), the Americana Music Association, the International Bluegrass Association, the Gospel Music Association, etc. Typically because having membership gave me access to the membership directory and I gained current contact information for independent artists, labels, and producers.

Some of my music publisher and songwriting friends have hired what are termed as "song pluggers". These are well-connected individuals who review and accept songs to pitch to labels or artists for a monthly retainer or fee. They may also receive a small percentage of revenue if they secure a placement. Typically, a song plugger's share of revenue is exclusive to that particular placement and not a share of the publishing.

You can still pursue any of those traditional paths; however, today, many songwriters are seeking out alternative methods of placing their songs. Methods that often skip trying to get them recorded by an artist or heard by a producer or record label.

There is another aspect of traditional placement, which has become more common: become an artist. If you can sing, and enjoy spending many nights out performing, becoming a performer is a way to get your songs out there.

In fact, most current artists (the highest percentage in music history) are also songwriters. The result is less opportunity for songwriters to place songs with the singer/songwriter artist.

Thinking Outside the Box

Some of the traditional methods I mentioned may still have relative success or value, mostly with independent artists or small independent record labels. However, today's songwriters are bypassing, or at least less dependent on, traditional methods of song placement. They have realized there are many opportunities to do something with their songs by getting out of the box.

Here are some placement outlets today's songwriters are utilizing:

YouTube
YouTube has become a popular medium for everything creative. Songwriters are utilizing YouTube to gain exposure for their own creative works.

Create and develop your own YouTube channel. It will fit in with your other social media endeavors and can be a great tool for getting your songs heard, branding yourself, and building a fan following.

If you perform your own songs and capture that on video, that's great. If you don't perform or don't perform well, you need to network and know an aspiring singer who would be willing to perform your songs.

Again, do a little research on how to pull off the best video recording you can with what you have to work with. If your video has poor audio or visual quality, the response will also be poor.

If you have professional sounding demos, you can create lyric videos of your songs. If you're not very savvy on editing video, this will require you to put on your non-songwriter's hat, roll your sleeves up and learn something new.

You can also create a video collage using various video clips and images that may tie into the theme of a song. Create your own four-minute movie with your song as the theme music. There are tons of websites out there that offer stock video footage for a small membership fee or for free. if you can't get stock footage or pay a videographer, shoot the footage yourself. Do your research in regard to best practices when shooting video, and make what you do look a good as it possibly can.

This can not only be a good way to gain exposure for your songs, it is a good test to see whether your songs will resonate with viewers.

One GRAMMY Award-winning artist recently recounted to me that a friend of his in an A&R position at a major label in New York will search through YouTube videos when he is looking for original material for his artists.

If you do create your own YouTube channel, you will also want to create a Google Adsense account and connect that to your YouTube channel so you possibly garner any ad revenue that may occur. Many major and independent labels earn revenue from ads that run on their YouTube channels and other outlets. In some cases, they earn more revenue than actually selling the music.

When creating any outlets like this, you not only want to think about exposure for potential song placements and building a fan following, but whether there is a possibility to monetize what you're doing.

Facebook

Facebook is a popular outlet not just for social media interaction, but for posting video as well. Chances are, you already have a personal Facebook page, but there are added benefits to creating a Facebook fan page as well. First and foremost, it's more professional. It's also better for branding yourself, and you can get a unique URL.

Many singer/songwriters develop a following through their Facebook fan pages by posting creative videos of their song performance directly to their Facebook fan page. It's a great way to capture shares and build your fanbase as a songwriter. If you're not a singer, have an aspiring singer perform your songs. This can work for both parties. If the song strikes a chord with Facebook followers, both of you gain exposure.

I recently created a Facebook video for a song in my publishing catalog that was a montage of pictures that supported the theme of the song. Because I've also networked and interacted through social media with radio personalities one of those radio personalities I've been friends with for years reached out and wanted an MP3 copy of the song to play on their FM Country station. The programmer also had me call in and conduct an interview about the song. Although I did get the exposure and interview, it took about two or three years of having an online relationship, and the message of the song striking a chord with them.

If you have been able to create great demos that have master recording quality, these are placements you can pursue.

TuneCore or CD Baby

If you read the demo section about recording demos of your songs, and you choose a path of creating demos that are also the equivalent of master recordings, another outlet to consider is actually releasing those songs as single releases or in a collect EP or album release.

Outlets such as TuneCore.com or CDBaby.com allow independent artists (or record labels, or anyone independent) to release their music to all digital outlets, including iTunes, Amazon.com and streaming services such as Spotify.

One bonus to using TuneCore is they offer a music publisher administration service (for a fee) that will collect additional revenues on the songs you release. TuneCore also has a creative services division to pitch song placements into TV, film, commercials, documentaries, etc.

I've personally had some success with master audio recordings in my publishing catalog using TuneCore.com.

They have made a few placements in documentaries of these songs.

If these are outlets you choose to pursue, make sure your music productions are commercially competitive.

SoundExchange.com
Should you make a choice to release your own recordings of your songs, you'll want to register with SoundExchange.com. SoundExchange is another performance rights organization, however they were created to collect digital royalties on behalf of performers and owners of master recordings.

Therefore if you are releasing recordings that you own and have paid to produce, you will want to make sure you have this area of potential revenue covered.

You will need to create an account with SoundExchange and provide a repertoire of all of your releases on the spreadsheet that SoundExchange provides. This is where good admin practices come into play because you'll need to know your release dates, UPC numbers, ISRC numbers, etc.

Taxi.com
Although I have not used Taxi.com, it is in essence a "song plugger" for produced music or music that is of the commercial quality of master recordings.

Taxi.com gives opportunities to songwriters and music creators by letting them know what placements are being sought after. Taxi submits songs to major and indie record labels, film & TV music supervisors, music publishers, production music libraries, TV commercials, video game companies and movie trailers. Taxi will screen submissions to see if it is on-target and great for the pitch and then submit it to the company that is searching for that particular style or genre.

Taxi.com does charge an annual fee for their service.

SoundCloud.com
SoundCloud is a great place to showcase your song demos. They have great features such as being able to easily obtain the embed codes for websites or for sharing on social media.

I personally use SoundCloud to post demos and email links to my personal contacts, or display my demo repertoire on my websites.

All Social Media Outlets
Don't neglect other social media outlets if you create a video or some type of social media marketing campaign for a song you've written.

From Twitter to Instagram, or whatever is the latest trending flavor of social media, become versed in how it works and how you can make it work for exposing your brand to a new audience. Build a following, as well as build your brand!

Radio

I've personally been a long-time user of AirPlayDirect.com. If you perform your own songs or have an independent artist you're working with record your songs, outlets such as AirPlayDirect.com is an economical way to make your songs available to radio programmers looking for independent material.

APD is used by many Bluegrass, Traditional Country and Americana programmers as well as some college stations and many overseas radio stations looking for new music .

For Pop or Electronic Music or other forms I've used entities such as ipluggers.com.

There are many outlets available like this, just do your research before paying any fees or releasing any of your music to make sure they do reach radio programmers.

With most of these types of outlets, you have access to reports that let you know which radio programmers have downloaded your music. Thus you can obtain more branding fodder for websites and social media outlets as you continue to build your brand.

Coordinate The Outlets
Be sure and have your ducks in a row if you choose to take on a campaign for placing your song.

For example, I co-wrote a song with Brad Davis called "Rock Star Zombie Killer". It was a bit unique and we didn't really have a clear placement for it. We created a lyric video that we posted to YouTube and Brad's Facebook fan page, then made the song available on AirplayDirect.com. We also paid a minimal fee for a campaign on ipluggers.com.

We had college radio stations add the song to their playlist and through ipluggers.com we had 60 radio programmers add the song across Europe.

You do not need your favorite artist to record your song. Become the brand ambassador for each individual song, and think outside the box on what you can do with it. No matter how great or small, every act you take builds your brand.

Build Your Online Presence
The first thing anyone does today when they meet someone or read something about them online is to "Google them" to find out more information.

If you were Googled right now, what would show up? Or would you show up at all?

It isn't just an added benefit to your brand if your name and image shows up in search engine results, it is a necessity.

You must carefully cultivate your brand and create a professional online presence. I put emphasis on carefully, because in all that you undertake you want to appear professional and reflect your brand in the best possible light.

There are two issues I see over and over again with aspiring songwriters. They either have little or no online presence, or what online presence they do have looks very unprofessional.

Once again, you will need to take off your songwriter hat and approach this as if you were working to brand or launch an artist. Consider all the things you would do if you were wanting to brand an artist, create online imaging, and marketing exposure.

The old school formula for Nashville songwriters was to perform at songwriter nights. Some of those places have become legendary, like The Bluebird Cafe. Songwriters would also find local hangouts to network with other songwriters.

Although these were effective in the past, I don't see much value for aspiring songwriters today. There is more value in getting a picture of yourself performing and posting it on social media than by what you can accomplish by attending.

Years ago I performed at the Bluebird Cafe. It was kind of a bucket list thing for me. I went early, signed up, waited my turn among dozens of other writers, got up and sang my song, and left. I did NOT get a picture!

I probably invested four hours that evening. Do you know what you can do in four hours? Learn how to launch a Wordpress website. Learn more about social media and how to reach people. Learn about video editing.

My point is, the Bluebird Cafe holds about 90-100 people. That took 4 hours of my total time that evening. Today, you can invest 4 hours into something else, launch it online and reach many more people in that manner and build your brand.

Now, if you love to get out and perform or just go hang out at places, by all means go do it. I'm not saying it's a negative, what I am saying is the value isn't what it used to be in furthering your songwriter career. And if you ever perform at the Bluebird Cafe, get a picture!

As you work on building your online presence and your brand, there is one piece of advice I would recommend (and this applies to songwriters, artists, producers, or anyone creative.)

Always cultivate the ability to emotionally step outside of yourself and view what you do with an objective, non-partial view.

Songwriters, as with any creative person, can get tunnel vision. It is easy to get caught up on one song or one aspect of what they're doing. Building an online presence is going to require you to take a 50,000 foot view of your brand.

Brands are built over long periods of time by putting multiple pieces of a puzzle together.

Think in broad terms of how to use search engines for keywords or phrases you want to be associated with. Learn how you can have your brand show up in those search results. Learn how can you target certain regions, genres, themes, demographics, etc.?

You can secure a domain name that either uses your own name or something creative that reflects your brand. The annual cost for a domain name can range from $8 - $15. You can also find free hosting for a basic website, and many website hosts also offer website templates that are easy to populate with your information.

Creating your own website is relatively inexpensive. The biggest key is having the knowledge. Knowledge can be obtained online by anyone in this day and time. There are tons of instructional YouTube videos available, usually by a 14-year-old guru!

Utilize a website style that is friendly to weekly or bi-weekly blogs posts or article posts. Plan out and schedule a variety of future blogs or posts. Create a Behind-The-Song blog once a month to highlight one of your songs, tell the backstory of how it was written. If you don't have a demo posted, post the lyric in the blog.

If you are a singer/songwriter and you do play some venues, get some pics and write a blog just as if you were music reporter covering a story.

Share something inspirational through a blog. You website needs to be an organic, living site with new content popping up several times a month.

Of course when you start having song placements, or you launch some campaign on YouTube or Facebook or whatever you do, be sure and create a post or blog on your website.

Learn all you can about search engine optimization, Wordpress has great plugins that check this for you. Learn about alt meta descriptions for your images and keywords to use to help them show up in Google searches.

You don't have to wait until you have ten or twenty song placements to begin to build your brand, to share your story, or let them know who you are. It's all part of building your brand.

Tie your website in with all of your social media platforms. Keep your content consistent across all of your platforms.

Twenty years ago, a songwriter's best chance of branding was having some great song placements or hits. They depended on a few select outlets: record labels, artists and producers.

Today the world is literally at your fingertips to build your brand. If you are writing songs, you're a songwriter. You can build your brand before you ever have your first song placed. You can share your songwriting products directly with others.

It's a great day and time with a vast amount of tools available. Utilize every component of building your presence online that you can.

The Little Things
There's a rule I've learned over the years that is a long-term key to living life. It applies to the music business as well. That rule is to always be mindful of the little things.

The fact is that it is not one big stage or grand event that creates or launches success. Just about everyone I know that became successful got up each and every day and did the little things. The boring, tedious, mundane little things over and over again.

It is the daily and weekly task of just doing the little things consistently year in and year out that leads to most people being viewed as "overnight sensations". There are no overnight sensations!

I've worked in the music business and have known people for decades, from the time I started to make friends and meet people to the present. I have watched some of their careers and have seen many go from just plugging away each day at the little things, to seeing them eventually become a success in their field.

The old adage of "the devil is in the details" is true. If you're not willing to commit to the details each and every day for years, you can't expect success.

To be honest, each song typically has a 3-5 year track before you see any results in regard to a significant placement. I've had songs that have been around for 10-15 years before they were placed.

I've known songwriters who 25 years ago were waiting tables at a restaurant and in their spare time were writing songs, creating demos and sending out pitch after pitch. Over the years they'd get a few small placements here and there. Some eventually landed big placements that changed their lives, but those placements didn't come without getting up each day and being attentive to the little things.

It's going to be the little things you do, day in and day out, that will build your brand as a songwriter. It's the small things you do day after day in attempting to place a song, or the little out-of-the-box marketing ideas or social media campaigns that will add up.

Don't neglect anything as being too small of a task to be attentive to in your pursuit in building your brand and placing your songs. The tiniest thing such as posting an inspiring quote on your social media not only will inspire others, but keep you inspired. It's ALL a part of your brand.

Always be open to learning new things, little by little. I've learned many new things over the years, and all of them have supported building my brand in some form or fashion.

The little things put into practice on a daily basis, whether in life or business, have the largest long term impact.

This is a rule that requires great trust. It's a rule for growth and success. The kind of growth you can't readily observe after a month or six months or even longer. I've seen too many examples in the lives of others, and my own life to know that it does work. You must trust the rule, even without immediate results.

There are no short-cuts, secrets, or magic answers to building something.

I used to consider myself a piano player. For a brief period in my life I thought I wanted to be a studio musician, until I worked around studio musicians that were A-list players.

They make what they do look easy and fun, what's not fun about a hot lead solo? Yet, they spent hours, weeks, months and years to be good at what they do. Hours of playing scales to a metronome to condition themselves to have perfect tempo. Moving the beats-per-minute up or down and running those scales all over again with various tempos, learning to hit every note in perfect time to the beat.

What a seemingly insignificant, tiny, boring task to do!

Little things tend to appear insignificant. They can be boring. They tend to not have any glamour or glitz. They may not be fun. They may require training yourself to develop new habits, but little things are the foundation of success.

Make it a habit to do the little things each and every week. The little things DO lead to bigger and better things down the road!

Chapter 20: Song Outlets – Get Out Of The Box!

The Tried and True Methods
The traditional path of a songwriter has been to pitch their songs to artists, record labels and producers. Another pursuit has been to collaborate with writers who have a larger network of contacts in the hopes of getting a song placed through a co-write.

If you wish to incorporate these traditional methods in order to place songs, you can seek out various organizations or entities that may aid you in your quest.

For example, I've had a RowFax.com membership in the past. Each week or month they listed not only major Country labels or artists that were looking for songs, but many of the independent artists and labels as well.

In conjunction with that, I've had memberships with the Country Music Association (CMA), the Americana Music Association, the International Bluegrass Association, the Gospel Music Association, etc. Typically because having membership gave me access to the membership directory and I gained current contact information for independent artists, labels, and producers.

Some of my music publisher and songwriting friends have hired what are termed as "song pluggers". These are well-connected individuals who review and accept songs to pitch to labels or artists for a monthly retainer or fee. They may also receive a small percentage of revenue if they secure a placement. Typically, a song plugger's share of revenue is exclusive to that particular placement and not a share of the publishing.

You can still pursue any of those traditional paths; however, today, many songwriters are seeking out alternative methods of placing their songs. Methods that often skip trying to get them recorded by an artist or heard by a producer or record label.

There is another aspect of traditional placement, which has become more common: become an artist. If you can sing, and enjoy spending many nights out performing, becoming a performer is a way to get your songs out there.

In fact, most current artists (the highest percentage in music history) are also songwriters. The result is less opportunity for songwriters to place songs with the singer/songwriter artist.

Thinking Outside the Box
Some of the traditional methods I mentioned may still have relative success or value, mostly with independent artists or small independent record labels. However, today's songwriters are bypassing, or at least less dependent on, traditional methods of song placement. They have realized there are many opportunities to do something with their songs by getting out of the box.

Here are some placement outlets today's songwriters are utilizing:

YouTube

YouTube has become a popular medium for everything creative. Songwriters are utilizing YouTube to gain exposure for their own creative works.

Create and develop your own YouTube channel. It will fit in with your other social media endeavors and can be a great tool for getting your songs heard, branding yourself, and building a fan following.

If you perform your own songs and capture that on video, that's great. If you don't perform or don't perform well, you need to network and know an aspiring singer who would be willing to perform your songs.

Again, do a little research on how to pull off the best video recording you can with what you have to work with. If your video has poor audio or visual quality, the response will also be poor.

If you have professional sounding demos, you can create lyric videos of your songs. If you're not very savvy on editing video, this will require you to put on your non-songwriter's hat, roll your sleeves up and learn something new.

You can also create a video collage using various video clips and images that may tie into the theme of a song. Create your own four-minute movie with your song as the theme music. There are tons of websites out there that offer stock video footage for a small membership fee or for free. if you can't get stock footage or pay a videographer, shoot the footage yourself. Do your research in regard to best practices when shooting video, and make what you do look a good as it possibly can.

This can not only be a good way to gain exposure for your songs, it is a good test to see whether your songs will resonate with viewers.

One GRAMMY Award-winning artist recently recounted to me that a friend of his in an A&R position at a major label in New York will search through YouTube videos when he is looking for original material for his artists.

If you do create your own YouTube channel, you will also want to create a Google Adsense account and connect that to your YouTube channel so you possibly garner any ad revenue that may occur. Many major and independent labels earn revenue from ads that run on their YouTube channels and other outlets. In some cases, they earn more revenue than actually selling the music.

When creating any outlets like this, you not only want to think about exposure for potential song placements and building a fan following, but whether there is a possibility to monetize what you're doing.

Facebook

Facebook is a popular outlet not just for social media interaction, but for posting video as well. Chances are, you already have a personal Facebook page, but there are added benefits to creating a Facebook fan page as well. First and foremost, it's more professional. It's also better for branding yourself, and you can get a unique URL.

Many singer/songwriters develop a following through their Facebook fan pages by posting creative videos of their song performance directly to their Facebook fan page. It's a great way to capture shares and build your fanbase as a songwriter. If you're not a singer, have an aspiring singer perform your songs. This can work for both parties. If the song strikes a chord with Facebook followers, both of you gain exposure.

I recently created a Facebook video for a song in my publishing catalog that was a montage of pictures that supported the theme of the song. Because I've also networked and interacted through social media with radio personalities one of those radio personalities I've been friends with for years reached out and wanted an MP3 copy of the song to play on their FM Country station. The programmer also had me call in and conduct an interview about the song. Although I did get the exposure and interview, it took about two or three years of having an online relationship, and the message of the song striking a chord with them.

If you have been able to create great demos that have master recording quality, these are placements you can pursue.

TuneCore or CD Baby

If you read the demo section about recording demos of your songs, and you choose a path of creating demos that are also the equivalent of master recordings, another outlet to consider is actually releasing those songs as single releases or in a collect EP or album release.

Outlets such as TuneCore.com or CDBaby.com allow independent artists (or record labels, or anyone independent) to release their music to all digital outlets, including iTunes, Amazon.com and streaming services such as Spotify.

One bonus to using TuneCore is they offer a music publisher administration service (for a fee) that will collect additional revenues on the songs you release. TuneCore also has a creative services division to pitch song placements into TV, film, commercials, documentaries, etc.

I've personally had some success with master audio recordings in my publishing catalog using TuneCore.com. They have made a few placements in documentaries of these songs.

If these are outlets you choose to pursue, make sure your music productions are commercially competitive.

SoundExchange.com
Should you make a choice to release your own recordings of your songs, you'll want to register with SoundExchange.com. SoundExchange is another

performance rights organization, however they were created to collect digital royalties on behalf of performers and owners of master recordings. Therefore if you are releasing recordings that you own and have paid to produce, you will want to make sure you have this area of potential revenue covered.

You will need to create an account with SoundExchange and provide a repertoire of all of your releases on the spreadsheet that SoundExchange provides. This is where good admin practices come into play because you'll need to know your release dates, UPC numbers, ISRC numbers, etc.

Taxi.com
Although I have not used Taxi.com, it is in essence a "song plugger" for produced music or music that is of the commercial quality of master recordings.

Taxi.com gives opportunities to songwriters and music creators by letting them know what placements are being sought after. Taxi submits songs to major and indie record labels, film & TV music supervisors, music publishers, production music libraries, TV commercials, video game companies and movie trailers. Taxi will screen submissions to see if it is on-target and great for the pitch and then submit it to the company that is searching for that particular style or genre.

Taxi.com does charge an annual fee for their service.

SoundCloud.com

SoundCloud is a great place to showcase your song demos. They have great features such as being able to easily obtain the embed codes for websites or for sharing on social media.

I personally use SoundCloud to post demos and email links to my personal contacts, or display my demo repertoire on my websites.

All Social Media Outlets
Don't neglect other social media outlets if you create a video or some type of social media marketing campaign for a song you've written.

From Twitter to Instagram, or whatever is the latest trending flavor of social media, become versed in how it works and how you can make it work for exposing your brand to a new audience. Build a following, as well as build your brand!

Radio
I've personally been a long-time user of AirPlayDirect.com. If you perform your own songs or have an independent artist you're working with record your songs, outlets such as AirPlayDirect.com is an economical way to make your songs available to radio programmers looking for independent material.

APD is used by many Bluegrass, Traditional Country and Americana programmers as well as some college stations and many overseas radio stations looking for new music .

For Pop or Electronic Music or other forms I've used entities such as ipluggers.com.

There are many outlets available like this, just do your research before paying any fees or releasing any of your music to make sure they do reach radio programmers.

With most of these types of outlets, you have access to reports that let you know which radio programmers have downloaded your music. Thus you can obtain more branding fodder for websites and social media outlets as you continue to build your brand.

Coordinate The Outlets
Be sure and have your ducks in a row if you choose to take on a campaign for placing your song.

For example, I co-wrote a song with Brad Davis called "Rock Star Zombie Killer". It was a bit unique and we didn't really have a clear placement for it. We created a lyric video that we posted to YouTube and Brad's Facebook fan page, then made the song available on AirplayDirect.com. We also paid a minimal fee for a campaign on ipluggers.com.

We had college radio stations add the song to their playlist and through ipluggers.com we had 60 radio programmers add the song across Europe.

You do not need your favorite artist to record your song. Become the brand ambassador for each individual song, and think outside the box on what you can do with it. No matter how great or small, every act you take builds your brand.

CHAPTER 21: BUILD YOUR ONLINE PRESENCE

The first thing anyone does today when they meet someone or read something about them online is to "Google them" to find out more information.

If you were Googled right now, what would show up? Or would you show up at all?

It isn't just an added benefit to your brand if your name and image shows up in search engine results, it is a necessity.

You must carefully cultivate your brand and create a professional online presence. I put emphasis on carefully, because in all that you undertake you want to appear professional and reflect your brand in the best possible light.

There are two issues I see over and over again with aspiring songwriters. They either have little or no online presence, or what online presence they do have looks very unprofessional.

Once again, you will need to take off your songwriter hat and approach this as if you were working to brand or launch an artist. Consider all the things you would do if you were wanting to brand an artist, create online imaging, and marketing exposure.

The old school formula for Nashville songwriters was to perform at songwriter nights. Some of those places have become legendary, like The Bluebird Cafe. Songwriters would also find local hangouts to network with other songwriters.

Although these were effective in the past, I don't see much value for aspiring songwriters today. There is more value in getting a picture of yourself performing and posting it on social media than by what you can accomplish by attending.

Years ago I performed at the Bluebird Cafe. It was kind of a bucket list thing for me. I went early, signed up, waited my turn among dozens of other writers, got up and sang my song, and left. I did NOT get a picture!

I probably invested four hours that evening. Do you know what you can do in four hours? Learn how to launch a Wordpress website. Learn more about social media and how to reach people. Learn about video editing.

My point is, the Bluebird Cafe holds about 90-100 people. That took 4 hours of my total time that evening. Today, you can invest 4 hours into something else, launch it online and reach many more people in that manner and build your brand.

Now, if you love to get out and perform or just go hang out at places, by all means go do it. I'm not saying it's a negative, what I am saying is the value isn't what it used to be in furthering your songwriter career. And if you ever perform at the Bluebird Cafe, get a picture!

As you work on building your online presence and your brand, there is one piece of advice I would recommend (and this applies to songwriters, artists, producers, or anyone creative.)

Always cultivate the ability to emotionally step outside of yourself and view what you do with an objective, non-partial view.

Songwriters, as with any creative person, can get tunnel vision. It is easy to get caught up on one song or one aspect of what they're doing. Building an online presence is going to require you to take a 50,000 foot view of your brand.

Brands are built over long periods of time by putting multiple pieces of a puzzle together.

Think in broad terms of how to use search engines for keywords or phrases you want to be associated with. Learn how you can have your brand show up in those search results. Learn how can you target certain regions, genres, themes, demographics, etc.?

You can secure a domain name that either uses your own name or something creative that reflects your brand. The annual cost for a domain name can range from $8 - $15. You can also find free hosting for a basic website, and many website hosts also offer website templates that are easy to populate with your information.

Creating your own website is relatively inexpensive. The biggest key is having the knowledge. Knowledge can be obtained online by anyone in this day and time. There are tons of instructional YouTube videos available, usually by a 14-year-old guru!

Utilize a website style that is friendly to weekly or bi-weekly blogs posts or article posts. Plan out and schedule a variety of future blogs or posts. Create a Behind-The-Song blog once a month to highlight one of your songs, tell the backstory of how it was written. If you don't have a demo posted, post the lyric in the blog.

If you are a singer/songwriter and you do play some venues, get some pics and write a blog just as if you were music reporter covering a story.

Share something inspirational through a blog. You website needs to be an organic, living site with new content popping up several times a month.

Of course when you start having song placements, or you launch some campaign on YouTube or Facebook or whatever you do, be sure and create a post or blog on your website.

Learn all you can about search engine optimization, Wordpress has great plugins that check this for you. Learn about alt meta descriptions for your images and keywords to use to help them show up in Google searches.

You don't have to wait until you have ten or twenty song placements to begin to build your brand, to share your story, or let them know who you are. It's all part of building your brand.

Tie your website in with all of your social media platforms. Keep your content consistent across all of your platforms.

Twenty years ago, a songwriter's best chance of branding was having some great song placements or hits. They depended on a few select outlets: record labels, artists and producers.
Today the world is literally at your fingertips to build your brand. If you are writing songs, you're a songwriter. You

can build your brand before you ever have your first song placed. You can share your songwriting products directly with others.

It's a great day and time with a vast amount of tools available. Utilize every component of building your presence online that you can.

Chapter 22: The Little Things

There's a rule I've learned over the years that is a long-term key to living life. It applies to the music business as well. That rule is to always be mindful of the little things.

The fact is that it is not one big stage or grand event that creates or launches success. Just about everyone I know that became successful got up each and every day and did the little things. The boring, tedious, mundane little things over and over again.

It is the daily and weekly task of just doing the little things consistently year in and year out that leads to most people being viewed as "overnight sensations". There are no overnight sensations!

I've worked in the music business and have known people for decades, from the time I started to make friends and meet people to the present. I have watched some of their careers and have seen many go from just plugging away each day at the little things, to seeing them eventually become a success in their field.

The old adage of "the devil is in the details" is true. If you're not willing to commit to the details each and every day for years, you can't expect success.

To be honest, each song typically has a 3-5 year track before you see any results in regard to a significant placement. I've had songs that have been around for 10-15 years before they were placed.

I've known songwriters who 25 years ago were waiting tables at a restaurant and in their spare time were writing songs, creating demos and sending out pitch after pitch. Over the years they'd get a few small placements here and there. Some eventually landed big placements that changed their lives, but those placements didn't come without getting up each day and being attentive to the little things.

It's going to be the little things you do, day in and day out, that will build your brand as a songwriter. It's the small things you do day after day in attempting to place a song, or the little out-of-the-box marketing ideas or social media campaigns that will add up.

Don't neglect anything as being too small of a task to be attentive to in your pursuit in building your brand and placing your songs. The tiniest thing such as posting an inspiring quote on your social media not only will inspire others, but keep you inspired. It's ALL a part of your brand.

Always be open to learning new things, little by little. I've learned many new things over the years, and all of them have supported building my brand in some form or fashion.

The little things put into practice on a daily basis, whether in life or business, have the largest long term impact.

This is a rule that requires great trust. It's a rule for growth and success. The kind of growth you can't readily observe after a month or six months or even longer. I've seen too many examples in the lives of others, and my own life to know that it does work. You must trust the rule, even without immediate results.

There are no short-cuts, secrets, or magic answers to building something.

I used to consider myself a piano player. For a brief period in my life I thought I wanted to be a studio musician, until I worked around studio musicians that were A-list players.

They make what they do look easy and fun, what's not fun about a hot lead solo? Yet, they spent hours, weeks, months and years to be good at what they do. Hours of playing scales to a metronome to condition themselves to have perfect tempo. Moving the beats-per-minute up or down and running those scales all over again with various tempos, learning to hit every note in perfect time to the beat. What a seemingly insignificant, tiny, boring task to do!

Little things tend to appear insignificant. They can be boring. They tend to not have any glamour or glitz. They may not be fun. They may require training yourself to develop new habits, but little things are the foundation of success.

Make it a habit to do the little things each and every week. The little things DO lead to bigger and better things down the road!

Chapter 23: More Tips

Types of Songs

When you're listening to a song that has become a hit, one of the key things you'll notice is how that song will typically contain well-written set lyrics along with an often unforgettable melody. Having said that the thing you may not become immediately aware of is how the song is structured. You see professional songwriters when writing a song take into consideration the genre of which the song is written for and the structure that will best suit the song. Now while there are several types of song forms, we're going to take a look at the most common forms used to give you a general idea.

The AAA Song Type

The AAA which is best known as the one-part song form is generally used when writing folk or country music. This song type generally does not have a bridge or chorus but instead consists of a number of verses. Nonetheless AAA type songs will often include a refrain in which a line is repeated at the closing of every verse.

Its like that song written by Simon and Garfunkel called "Bridge over Troubled Water". If you were to closely look at the lyrics of the song you will notice that three of the verses used in the song contain a number of lines. Each of the written verses are different in the structure of their lyrics and in the final verse there's a variation in the melody. Notice how the line "Like a bridge over troubled water" is repeated at the end of each verse.

The AABA Song Type

Songs written using the AABA form will have an opening section, followed by a bridge and then transitioning to a final segment. Hence AABA where A is the opening, and B the bridge. You'll often see this song type used in variety of genres such as jazz, gospel, and even pop-music.

The Verse/Chorus Song Type

You'll mostly see this song type used in most love songs, rock and roll, country and pop-music. Popular songs such as "I Wanna Dance With Somebody" written by the late Whitney Houston and "Material Girl" by Madonna have both utilized this particular song form.

Before we continue to the next chapter I would like to share one important tip for you to remember whenever you're writing the chorus or verse of your song;

Always avoid writing verses that are too lengthly and try to get to the chorus quickly.

If you want to use a perfect example, just listen to the song "More Than Just The Two Of Us" written by the group Sneaker. The song contains three verses with a chorus following the end of each verse. This is what is known as creating a memorable effect.

Verse 1- There are times when all of your love is meant for me

Chorus – It's more than just the two of us

Verse 2 – In your touch come the words so hard to say

Chorus – It's more than just the two of us

Final Verse – in my eyes you are the warmth of the sun

Chorus repeated twice – Its more than just the two of us

Do you see that?

Great songwriters will use what most songwriters like to refer to as song art which allows their songs to have an emotional impact on the listener allowing for a memorable experience. This technique used by many songwriters and often referred to as a "song craft" are subjective and weren't thought up as some scheme to drive the songwriter out of their minds trying to create a recipe for a song without originality or depth. Song craft was developed over centuries of songwriting by songwriters who realized that they needed to find ways of allowing the listeners to not only understand what their songs were saying, but also to share the experience and remember the message conveyed at the heart of the song.

From the opening lines of the first verse to the final chorus of your song your listeners should feel as though they are being taken along on a journey that touches their deepest emotions or make them feel as though they are compelled to leap onto the dance floor and express themselves screaming "Thats My Jam". What you don't want as a songwriter is to end up writing one of those songs which makes the listener feel like they're wandering in the desert totally frustrated and waiting to be put out of their misery. Most listeners when exposed to a such a song will just tune themselves out. This book is specifically tailored to prevent you from falling in such a trap. In the next chapters I will share with you some simple yet powerful techniques to write songs to create the perfect listening experience not only for your listeners but also yourself. However like any developed skill perfecting the song craft takes some practice and effort on your part.

Do You Write the Lyrics Before or After the Music?

Ok so what do I do....what do I do first? Music, Lyrics, Lyrics Music...ugh! Yup that was me just a few years ago when planning to write my first song. Sound familiar? One of the most challenging tasks in songwriting is getting started. That's right. Not only is it the most difficult aspect of songwriting but it's also the most important. But don't worry. Once you're able to overcome this hurdle, it's relatively smooth sailing from there. Well not totally smooth but a lot less trouble as you'll now know where you're headed and you'll now have a lot more to say.

Now just as I was; you're going to be tempted to charge in and begin writing your song with the first thought that crosses your mind. Don't. You already know you want to write a song using some lyrics a melody and a harmonic note. However chances are you may by unclear of the feeling you want to express with your listeners. When this happens you run the risk of ending up writing a song your listeners will not be able to neither relate to nor understand.

You've heard them before. Its that song that no matter how many times you listen to it, you always end up saying in the end "What the hell was that guy singing about?"

Well where should you begin;

(a) melody or

(b) lyrics?

The Answer: (c) None of the above.

Not what you were expecting right? Lets continue.

It's true that there are several ways for you to begin writing your song but before you even consider the lyrics or melody I suggest you start with giving your song a title.

The title of your song is what your listeners will remember your song by, especially if its a hit single or number one on the Top 100 Billboard Charts. Not to mention that the title of your song will be the defining factor used to convey the message you want to share with your listeners. Think of it as your guide to allowing you to maintain a level of focus to keep you on the right track to guarantee that you are able to achieve the undivided attention of your listeners whenever your song is being played. I often like to use the analogy of the title of my song as the roof of my house with the walls, foundation and supporting building structure as the rest of the song.

Using a short but catchy phrase makes for a great song title because they'll often grab the attention of the listener and of course they'll be much more easier to remember than some long and uninterested and cumbersome name. So limit the title for your song to about five or six words.

Always choose a song title that appeals to you. It should be a phrase that rings something true the minute you hear it. It's something that your listeners when hearing the title will say to themselves, "I've got to see what that song is about". And guess what. Once you're able to peak the interest of one listener; others will want to know more too. And so it begins

Finding a Great Title For Your Song.

Always be on the lookout for good titles that may catch your attention. Short phrases, images and action words generally make a good title for your song. Did you know that many of the newspaper headlines can be used to choose a great title for your song? Just look at few I came across during the last couple of weeks: "A Vision On The Edge", "Basking in the Shadows" and "Drifting Away". And yes feel free to use any of them.

You can also listen to your inner self by doing a bit of creative writing. Just type the first thing that comes to mind as fast as you can, then look back and see if you can find any creative phrases you could use for your the title of your song. I've found that by watching television I have often been able to come up with some catchy little phrase I was able to use for the title of my song. Listening in to a random conversation when riding the train home from work, listening to the radio while driving home in your car or even something that catches your attention during that boring office meeting at work can offer the perfect song title. Get yourself a notepad and start keeping a record of these titles. You never know which one will be your next hit song.

Have you Started?

Well what are you waiting for?

Stop reading. Get a notebook or piece of paper, pick up the nearest magazine or newspaper right now and jot down at least five phrases that catch your attention. Mix them up a bit and include some of your own words. Spend a few minutes playing around with some ideas for creating catchy phrases and try to come up with at least two that you think will make great titles for your song.

TURN YOUR TITLE INTO LYRICS

Do you see why I needed you to find a title in Chapter 2 ? In this chapter we're now going to focus our attention in turning your title for your song into an extraordinary lyric by asking ourselves a few simple questions. Well actually questions which are suggestive of your chosen title. Using these questions as an usher to write the lyrics to your song you'll not only complete just about every song you begin writing and keep the listeners interested from start to finish. But you will also be able to effectively use your song to carry your message to the listener making your song say just about anything you want it to.
Lets look at the questions behind the title.

Every title for every song suggests a number of answerable questions. Some of these questions will be directed towards yourself while others will be specifically aimed at the listeners. Nonetheless you the songwriter will need to have the answers to them both. Let's look at a few songs.

Have you ever listened to the timeless song "Heartbreak Hotel" and asked yourself What goes on at this "Heartbreak Hotel"? Where is this hotel? And How can I get there?

Well guess what. Although it may sound unrealistic there are actually valid answers to each of those questions.

"Heartbreak Hotel" is that place you go when your wife or girlfriend leaves you.

"Heartbreak Hotel" is that place filled with tears from the cries of the saddened lovers.

You'll find "Heartbreak Hotel" at the corner of Lonely and Saddened Street.

Let's look at another example; "I Knew You Were Trouble" by Taylor Swift. Well can you possibly guess what the questions are? Let's see.

Who was the person giving all this trouble?, What were they doing?, and Did things ever work out? Now if the song doesn't offer any answers, you'll only end up with a disappointed listener. It just like watching that great mystery movie or reading an intriguing novel and not finding out who was committing all the murders.

Whenever I listen to Trace Adkins Country hit "You're Gonna Miss This" the first question I'm always asking, and I mean every single time is What am I going to miss? Heehaw and Why am I going to miss it? Ok let me get my mind out of the gutter. If you listen closely to the lyrics of the song you will be blown away by the answer. Now that there is the making of a GREAT song and one you should emulate. It captivates your interest with the questions and offers the answers in an innovative way.

You may even choose the questions you would like to answer. However you'll need to ensure that the questions asked will also be those which are asked by the listeners who will also arrive at the same answers. Take this approach and ask yourself; "If I were the listener what would I want to know when listening to this song?

Take a look at these questions which I have found offered me with some great song titles.

What does the title of the song mean?

How do I feel about the title?

What was the reason behind the title?

What would I like to see happen next?

Try it.

Take a look back at your title you created in Chapter 2 and ask yourself the suggested questions I just listed and make a list of the answers. The answers you're able to come up with will be those which you'll want to include in the lyrics of your song. Now taking it from a listeners perspective, add a few more questions you would ask if you were the listener. Are they going to understand the title of your song? Will you have to explain what your title means?

Begin by telling the listener why you're writing the song. You can start off by writing down a few answers to those questions. Don't try to think about whether the words rhyme or not. We're not focusing on that right now, nor are we thinking about it as writing the lyrics of the song. Right now all we're doing is just answering a few questions. It is by you taking this approach that you'll be able to create the heart of your song which will touch the lives of your listeners.

Use Your Motivation To Bring Your Song To Life

You know how Michelangelo uses his paint to create his world renown master pieces. Well every songwriter included yourself has a group of images, original concepts and influential words used to create a hit song. I like to call these our raw materials. And it is with these raw materials you are going to create your first hit song by utilizing the phrases, words and images recommended by the title of your song.

Let's assume that the title for your song is "Baby You Make Me Happy". It we're going to create a list of raw materials on the basis of this title, the first thing we're going to do is start thinking of the words and thoughts commonly associated with a person happy. We can begin with some general words such as smile. bright, funny and happy. These should probably be the words you may want include in the lyrics of your song. However if you'll notice they do seem a bit non-pictorial don't you think? I'm sure if we put our heads together we can come up with some other words with which our listeners will be able to create a mental image of what the song is saying and share the experience with a smile or laugh.

Take for instance the word "fun". Some of the events often regarded as fun to make people smile include dancing, parties, or even going to the amusement park. So wouldn't it be fair for us to picture someone at a party dancing or at the amusement park riding a roller coaster?

I would like to consider these as just a couple basic ideas. Try not to decide whether they may be great ideas or not just yet. Instead just jot down anything which comes to mind. Even though you're probably not going to be able to use all of them you never know which ones might just end up in your hit song.

When I think of the word "shining" the first thing which comes to mind is sunny and I immediately start thinking of summer and the great outdoors filled with lush green grass, freshly scented flowers and tall trees. And when I think about the flowers I remember all the bright colors and the buzzing of the bees, the chirping of the birds and the colorful swarm of butterflies.

Can you see what we just did? Look Carefully.

Now we have some words which we can use to bring to the mind of the listeners mental images of flowers, sunshine, bees, roller coasters at the amusement park, parties and dancing. All these words are connected with a person smiling and having a great feeling. And guess what. All that came from the word "shining" and us using it's suggestive power.

If you want to know how you can use these words in a hit song, just listen to a section of Uncle Kracker's song "Smile". You make me dance like a fool, Oh, you make me smile and Buzz like a bee.

Can you see how the listener is able to create a mental image of the what the singer is experiencing instead of asking us to take him at his word. Considerably this is one of the most essential tools a songwriter could ever have. Check out this song by listening to it on Youtube and see how you'll better be able to visualize for yourself the images of someone smiling.

Once you've been able to make your list of accompanying words, make a list of words and images which are contrary to someone smiling. For instance. Lets say you're writing a song called "California Babe". Well if that were the title of your song you would want to use words such as water, summer, hot, waves, paradise and free. Now your contrasting works would be seen as words including cold, darkness, entrapment, and the moon. You can use this to add some more lyrics to your song.

FIND A STRUCTURE FOR YOUR SONG

Before we take another step it's important that we reacquaint ourselves with song structure. Remember we spoke about this in Chapter 1 of this book. A easily-followed song structure functions as a pathway guiding the listener through the song from start to finish maintaining the interest and attention of the person.
A typical song structure will often reflect the song having a verse followed by a chorus, then another verse, then the chorus again transitioning to a bridge and then closing with the chorus.

Most listeners will prefer this type of song because if offers a certain amount of repetition to maintain their interest and create a sense of familiarity in the song. Not to mention it also allows the songwriter (you) to add heart to your song. If you look at most of the hit songs today you'll notice a pattern of a conversational and informal verse followed by a dynamic chorus providing a melodramatic thump.

Take a look at these handy definitions you can use to grasp the concept of song structure

The Verse – All the verses in a song will generally have the same melody but varying lyrics. It is these lyrics which the songwriter will use to convey the necessary information and answer the relative questions about the title of the song, the people involved and the situation.

The Chorus of the Song – You'll probably hear the chorus of the song on three to four occasions. Each time the lyrics of the chorus will remain the same and will sum up the heart and emotions of the song. Often the title of the song will appear within the chorus and may even be repeated two to three times.

The Bridge – The bridge of the song uses a completely different melody and set of lyrics with a chord progression from either the verse or the chorus. The bridge of the song offers the songwriter an opportunity to break away from the repetitiveness of the verse and chorus while providing the listener with some insight to the story or message of the song.

Now look back at your previous questions and select an answer within each section. Remember, your chorus will be repeated two to three times so its important that you choose the question which is considered as a key question both you and the listener would like to have answered. And be sure to include the title of your song in the chorus.

FIND THE MELODY IN YOUR LYRICS

Did you know that every time you speak you're actually singing? It's true. Let's prove it. Just try speaking without changing your pitch, without increasing or decreasing the speed at which you're speaking or without elevating or lowering your voice. It's easy. Just pretend as though you're speaking like Microsoft Sam on the computer. Ah! Now you get it. Sounds robotic doesn't it. So if you were to really look at it we use a lot of melody in our voices whenever we're speaking. Don't we.

Whenever we speak we use a pitch, volume, a rhythmic pattern and phrasing. These are all general characteristics of a melody of a song. The difference however is, in your song these attributes are somewhat elevated and more often repeated. If you've got a few lyric lines to your song, all you'll need to do is speak them to acquire a basic melody going and provide some exaggeration to the pitches creating a rhythm to the words allowing any pauses to happen naturally.

Once you've achieved some melody to your lyrics take some time and begin roughing out the chords with your keyboard, guitar or any other musical instrument of your choice. Personally I have found it easier to record the vocals before adding any chords. This allows me to recall the original melody should I need to refer to it. Now bear in mind, there are other ways to write a great melody for your song but this method is one of the best ways to start. And I should know.

How to Improve Your Songwriting Skills

If you're thinking of finding a collaborator to add music to your lyrics then you should probably finish the lyrics before you start looking. It's going to be a challenge filling in the rest of the lyrics while maintaining an emotional tone but hey, the worst is already over. You can do it.

Try not to twist your words out of meaning just to achieve some rhythmic pattern to your words. A "vowel rhyme" will often rhyme such as sign, mine, time or love and enough with a similar vowel yet seen having different closing constants. Don't worry this generally works for most if not all songs. Songs for a musical theatre however are somewhat different and often require the lyrics to have a near perfect or perfect rhymes.

Don't work on your lyrics for extended time periods. If you've hit a stump in your lyrics there's no shame in walking away for a while. Be sure to keep the lyrics written down on a notepad or in a book so you can always reflect back on it when something new hits you. Try to keep the melody at the forefront of your mind and most importantly don't lose the heart of your song. Maintain a high standard of emotional content and whenever you feel as though you are loosing your way, stop working for a while and come back when you've rested. You'll be able to see more clearly what's needed to be done. You'll see. Just keep on working at it until you experience a genuine love and excitement fueling motivation for songwriting.

CHAPTER 24: FITTING IT IN AN HOUR

Writing a song in an hour is truly an amazing feat. Many artists spend weeks, months & sometimes even years (yes, I'm talking about Chinese Democracy), working on their songs and while the perfection will eventually pay off, the tunnel vision does create a lot of problems. Firstly, it blocks out an artist's creative scope and renders him/her unable to release anything until they're done with the previous task. But let's not get into artists at the moment. For now, assuming you're a beginner who wants to feel what it's like to be an artist, coming with songs in an hour would mark a major achievement. The method that I'm about to explain will enable you to write songs in under an hour, but do bear in mind that this wouldn't be the most perfect way of doing things. However, the practice will provide your creative barriers a big breakthrough and you'll actually develop greater interest in the whole songwriting process.

You will be aware of most of the processes involved in writing a song, so keep them in mind, and follow the techniques given below.

Lower your expectations

The practice may sound a little depressing, but the truth is that it will really help you deal with any kind of disappointment. Considering that you're a beginner or fairly new to the entire songwriting process, you shouldn't expect a Coldplay type hit out of your song. And you shouldn't feel down because right now hits are not what you're aiming for.

Instant Inspiration:

The clock's ticking and your countdown from an hour has begun. This means that you can't lose a grip on your timing indulging any self-mutilating activity like coming up with sensitively intense lyrics. So it's best to not overthink things right now; scan the newspaper if you have to, the TV headlines or a promo ad lying in the corner of your room. Just take anything, don't judge the pros & cons and start writing a song about it. In this one hour process, being picky is not an option.

Now, remember the techniques you were taught earlier, of managing things the right way. Have an idea file with you at all times, and who knows subconsciously your mind will keep throwing ideas at you all week, at work or at home. You need to note these ideas so when the time comes, you don't have to improvise that much, as described in the previous paragraph. And don't worry, you won't be overriding the one-hour time limit in any way since you won't be writing any lyric or melody during that time, just giving your observation a written meaning. Have an easily accessible idea file/drawer ready which will speed up the entire process greatly.

Just like clockwork:

Instant songwriting is not possible if you don't use a well-managed approach while writing the song. A cluttered & jumbled approach will mean that an hour alone will be spent bringing the components together. Furthermore, if you're a team and each member has been assigned a specific tasks, e.g. drums, bass, guitar, lyrics, etc. then working in collaboration will help you a lot as 2 minds are always better than one.

When the hour starts, everyone must be aware of their responsibilities. As a lyricist, you need to think of the theme of the song, its genre and the wanted outcome. If you keep on questioning your motives, then it's highly unlikely that you will make any progress. Plan the entire process by using a piece of paper and a pen, making a general guideline which should contain:

- ✓ The song's title,
- ✓ Its genre & style, don't worry about the music right now,
- ✓ All the components of the song, i.e. lyrics for every different musical instrument, if any.

In many bands, songwriter don't work on the song's structure until all the lyrics have been written but when producing an entire song in an hour, it is absolutely necessary that the lyricist, i.e. you, write the lyrics for each musician, if any. If there aren't any musicians and it's just you, then the entire process would become a whole lot simpler.

Spend no longer than 15 minutes on the process; with the passage of time you'll be able to reduce the time spent to a mere 5 minutes. Next, assign their respective tasks to everyone and you start out with the lyrics. The writing phase should be kept under 20 minutes; seems like a short time, doesn't it? Well, these 20 minutes will put a lot of stress on you, so you should keep a hold of your nerves during this time and never give up to the surrounding pressure.

The Lyricist's Job:

As a lyricist, the initial thing that you'll need will be a whole lot of writing material. Heaps to be exact! Note down every word & phrase combination that comes in your mind and once you've had plenty of these ideas noted down, start throwing them into meaningful (or semi-meaningful!), choruses & verses. Don't waste any time filtering out any lyrics that don't bring a smoothness to your ears because there's a deadline you need to stick to.

Coming up with lines in under 20 minutes is a doable task. No doubt, that the verses won't be poetic but short song of 2 verses, 1 chorus & a bridge can be completed within this time.

The Musician's Job:

Don't read this portion if you don't plan on making any melodies but I've provided this resource, just in case you decide to make the music as well. If you are looking to produce music in under an hour, then you must have prior knowledge of musical instruments because I really can't teach you how to play a musical instrument in an hour. Assuming that you know how to play an instrument try to develop a tune that fits the lyrics. Cluster together a number of melodies until you stumble onto something that really goes well with the lyrics. This won't take that long, given that you have knowledge of the instrument.

The first & foremost thing that you would want to produce would be a hook which can either be really simple or really complex, depending on your preference. The hook may be used as an intro, the music for the chorus or you can play with it around the bridge. Almost half of the musicians work will be done once he/she prepares a hook.

If you pay attention while listening to a song, you will notice that the hook introduces the song, from where it enters the chorus. If you want, you can make the music a little complex by adding in extra instruments, but I would recommend you to keep this at a minimum and focus on the lyrics.

But before I move on, I must say that if you know how to play guitar, then try to insert a guitar slow as part of the bridge into the song. This will add new life to your song and eliminate the need for a lyrical bridge as the void will be filled with the melody.

Structures:

Having a sense of structure when writing the song will reduce the time needed to write it. Making the shift from one temp to the other, or one key to the other will take time as heed must be given to make the transition as smooth as possible. To stay on safe side, especially because you have limited time, stick to your own timing & key. And if you feel as if the song is too boring then you can polish it a bit, as explained in the next chapter.

It's quite lucky for anyone writing a Western song as there are a limited number of song structures. I've prepared a list of templates so you'll have easy access to them.

1. The classic

✓ **Intro,**

✓ **Verse,**

✓ **Chorus,**

✓ **Verse,**

✓ **Chorus,**

2. The classic with a little twist

✓ **Intro,**

✓ **Verse,**

✓ **Chorus,**

✓ **Verse,**

✓ **Chorus,**

✓ **Bridge,**

✓ **Chorus,**

3. The double verse

- ✓ **Intro,**
- ✓ **Verse,**
- ✓ Instrumental break,
- ✓ **Verse,**
- ✓ **Chorus,**
- ✓ Guitar solo,
- ✓ **Chorus,**

4. The Hard Rock version

- ✓ **Intro,**
- ✓ **Verse,**
- ✓ **Chorus,**
- ✓ Tame guitar solo,
- ✓ **Verse,**
- ✓ **Chorus,**
- ✓ Epic guitar solo,
- ✓ **Chorus,**
- ✓ Long guitar solo outro,

Some musicians after tweaking with the structure found out that the following structure is the simplest one:

- ✓ **Intro,**
- ✓ **Verse,**
- ✓ **Break,**
- ✓ **Verse,**
- ✓ **Chorus,**
- ✓ **Bridge,**
- ✓ **Chorus,**
- ✓ **Solo,**
- ✓ Chorus & Outro

This setting may use up your entire mind & body and leave you with seconds to spare, but it will definitely give you a nice enough song worth being proud of. After a few practices, the time limit will force your creativity to work faster and you'll be able to produce songs at a much faster pace.

CHAPTER 25: POLISHING

Ever visited the beach? If you have, you must've seen a number of pebbles & rocks, some jagged up while others as rounded & smooth as they can be. These rounded pebbles weren't like this; they were rocks that were polished and smoothened by waves. In the same manner, the first time you write a song, it will have a number of problems in it, it won't be easy to listen or understand, but with the passage of time as you keep working on it, you'll have a well-polished piece.

Polishing is what truly brings out the best in a song, especially if it's been in a hurry. After listening to your song, you may feel proud but after 3 – 5 times, you'll ask yourself, "Is it really that great"?

So go back and take another look at the song you wrote. I'm not saying to get your head down on a song for months because you aren't a professional musician, but taking a look at it from different angles would surely help. If you think you're facing a stone wall during this process, then let it go for a few hours and come back to it later.

Ask yourself,

- Are the lyrics really conveying my thoughts in the most imaginative way possible?
- Can I add more color & description to the line?
- Have I provided well enough explanation to the scene?

- Have I added too many ands, buts, etc. to the verse?
- Am I repeating the same idea with different words in every line?
- Do I really need 3 choruses?
- Have I gotten my tenses & pronouns together?

Remember progression & freshness will be the key when polishing your song. Trim any fat off the song; one word can make all the difference in the world. Also, if you start writing a song in 1st person then don't make a sudden switch to 3rd person. If you include a melody, then make sure that it doesn't ascend when the lyrics are light and doesn't descent when the lyrics are sad. Polishing, rewriting, or rechecking your work is what will separate you from an unsuccessful songwriter. There is a possibility that hundreds of poorly written songs could have been hits if the writer was willing to give them another try.

The most common features of a poorly written song are:

- Predictability – a great song always manages to achieve a balance between surprise & predictability. Too much predictable content can be as damaging as too much surprise in the song will greatly dent the song's quality.
- Preaching – a message imparted in a subtle manner can be way too effective than one that drills right into your head. Listeners are quite frequently turned off by preaching and unless you're Bruce Springsteen, I advise you stay from this method!
- Self-pity – this practice must be avoided as much as possible, unless of course you're writing a blues song. Elements of self-pity in any other genre may sound

appealing to you but will be very boring to the general audience.
- Personal symbolism – once again, this skill needs some time to develop, so you shouldn't include it in your first few songs.
- Ornate language – if you're writing a funny song then ornate elements can surely be used to add a comic effect to the song, but remember that a song won't be a success if the audience's attention is used up, deciphering the flowery language.
- Generalization – people respond better to "to-the-point" & solid images rather than an overall idea.

It is vital that you remember that a song is not the same as a recording. Many people know this simple fact due to the great many number of hollow artists appearing in mainstream music on the basis of recording wizardry. No doubt that a great melody helps make the song successful, but remember that a good song will always stand out on its own & will have its own life. A hit song will focus on just one feeling and will illicit visual images in the listener's brain. The audience will find it very easy to relate to the song and will remain enthralled & engaged in it all the way to the end.

Don't write for yourself; write to communicate. Say what you want to say, as comprehensively as possible and don't oversell the idea.

Conclusion

It is always pleasing and soothing to listen to a beautiful song. The beauty of a song depends on many factors. The music plays an important part. The lyrics must be good naturally. Without good lyrics, it would be difficult for a music composer to express himself. When we say good lyrics, we do not mean grammatically correct words. Poetry does not care for grammar. You can twist the words and their meanings to convey what is in your heart. Songs are just an extended form of poetry.

There is one thing most artists will tell you; art can be very unpredictable in the way that inspiration is presented to you. Some of the best songs ever made started with lyrics that someone felt inspired to write, without even having a melody or song structure in mind, while others came after an entire song structure had been built.

Art is not meant to be bound by any rules, but there is no way to deny that some of those rules are very useful when creating a composition, and those rules will allow you to get optimal results as far as the engagement you get. This is the main reason so many artists will tell you their best compositions came with no regards to music theory or rules, while others came out of a structure created with musical theory.

Songwriting need not be scary. It can be quiet, intense, exciting, frustrating, and fulfilling all within the first five minutes. Remember to be patient with yourself – you're learning, after all – because you will get results if you stick with it, just like everything you try. Practice makes perfect, so take a moment to remember that, when you start to hate on yourself for an awkward phrase or structure. You can do this. Hopefully, these tips will help you, so you get the best results at a great speed that will amaze you.

Keep writing and never give up!

DISCOVER "HOW TO FIND YOUR SOUND"

HTTP://MUSICPROD.ONTRAPAGES.COM/

SWINDALI MUSIC COACHING/SKYPE LESSONS.

Email djswindali@gmail.com for info and pricing

Printed in Great Britain
by Amazon